GAA Fun & Games

Quotes, Jokes, Hits & Misses

GAA Fun & Games

Quotes, Jokes, Hits & Misses

JOHN SCALLY

WOLFHOUND PRESS

First published in 2007 by
Wolfhound Press
An imprint of Merlin Publishing
Newmarket Hall, St Luke's Avenue,
Cork Street, Dublin 8, Ireland
Tel: +353 1 4535866
Fax: +353 1 4535930
publishing@merlin.ie
www.merlinwolfhound.com

Text © 2007 John Scally
Editing, Design and Layout © 2007 Merlin Publishing

Cover image courtesy of Weeshie Fogarty, featuring his
Granddaughter Lucy.

13-Digit ISBN 978-0-86327-9478

A CIP catalogue record for this book is available from the British
Library.

10 9 8 7 6 5 4 3 2 1

Typeset & Design by Artwerk
Cover Design by Graham Thew Design
Printed and bound WS Bookwell, Finland

A heavy cloud of sadness came over me as this book was being written with the news of the death of one of Ireland's greatest footballers and captains, Jimmy Murray. I think the fact that he knew my grandfather, who died before I was born, cemented my affection for him. Like many other people from the West of Ireland I had experienced his great generosity at first hand.

Jimmy will forever remain a true GAA icon. The Sam Maguire trophy is a repository of secrets and dreams. Two of them are the best elegy. Memory is our way of holding on to those we love. Jimmy has left us a treasure trove of Croke Park memories.

Contents

Acknowledgements

My thanks to Joe Brolly, Dermot Earley, Ger Loughnane, Jimmy Magee, Joseph O'Connor, John O'Mahony, Sue Ramsbottom and Pat Spillane for their support and friendship and to the many other players, past and present, who shared their personal anecdotes, quotes, jokes, hits and misses with me.

Special thanks to my good friend Peter Woods for his practical assistance.

Also to Connell Doris who has journeyed bravely and with good humour as this book was being written.

Thanks to Chenile Keogh and Aoife Barrett and all at Wolfhound Press for their enthusiastic support of this book. My particular gratitude to my editor, former camoige star, Noelle Moran.

Introduction

Some people get totally out of shape when they retire from playing sport. Not so me. I was never in good shape in the first place. However, I am part of a chosen few. There are four types of people: happy people, sad people, very sad people and then people who collect funny sports quotations and stories. I belong to that endangered species.

First a few words of warning. There are books of truth. There are books of fact. This is not one of them. This will not be a publication for anoraks because my aim was neither veracity nor accuracy. My sole agenda was to try and put a smile on peoples' faces. I dedicated my time and energy to finding the funniest GAA quotations and anecdotes and where there were debates about who said what I focused on what was said rather than spending exhaustive research on who said it. In the case of the anecdotes though, all that has been changed is the facts! No story was too apocryphal for consideration if it was funny. My attitude was that if it was funny enough it just might be true enough!

Tribunal watchers reared on a diet of the truth, the whole truth and nothing but the truth will despair at this book because in this context it was humour that was sacrosanct. It is often said that truth is the first casualty of war. In some cases truth may have been a casualty; in these pages the agenda to entertain took precedence.

I feel the time is right for this book. I think back to my youth. During the glory days in the 1980s one of the players on the Kerry team, who must remain nameless, said during the League campaign: "Life isn't all beer and football. Some of us haven't touched a football in months." I loved the comment of the Offaly hurler, who must also remain nameless, the Friday before a Leinster hurling final against Kilkenny. "We're taking this match awful seriously. We're training three times a week now, and some of the boys are off the beer since Tuesday." There is not enough of that kind of craic and *joie de vivre* in Gaelic games today.

The great thing about the GAA is the passion it creates and this passion in turn generates many moments of comedy. It was personal experience that led me down this journey. After the 1996 and 1997 All-Irelands when Mayo let All-Ireland titles slip through their fingers Pat Spillane poured scorn on the Mayo forwards in particular. His comments were not appreciated in Mayo to such an extent that the mere mention of Spillane's name in Mayo was as welcome as a nun in a brothel.

The GAA fan's life is punctuated by moments of remembered blessings. One of the most memorable train journeys I have ever experienced was shortly after the 1997 All-Ireland. I found myself sitting beside a man of mature years, who was puffing away on his pipe. Given his disposition I thought at first he might be a parish priest. The conversation quickly turned to football and he gave an incisive critique of the problems of Connacht football. Then he turned to the media reportage of teams from the West. Immediately he had a transformation of Dr Jekyll and Mr Hyde proportions. He reeled off a litany of names of journalists and pundits and what he proposed to do with them cannot be reprinted on the grounds of public order and morality. After his vicious tirade he paused for deep breath. A pregnant pause ensued before he said more in sorrow than in anger, "F**k them all bar Spillane."

I nearly fell of my seat. I was wondering what he would say about the Kerry man that hadn't already been said about nuclear war. I heard myself ask incredulously, "Why do you say bar Spillane?"

"Ah sure, young fella, Spillane is f**ked already."

This book celebrates such comic creations. Appropriately it begins with that self-same Pat Spillane. Everybody who is anybody in Gaelic games is here from Christy Ring to Ger Loughnane; from Joe Brolly to Joe Kernan; from Babs Keating to Graham Geraghty; from John O'Mahony to John in the pub; from Angela Downey to Buffy the Vampire Slayer.

ONE

Pat on the Back

If someone said to me five years ago that I would become friends with Pat Spillane I would have laughed at them because where I come from in Roscommon they speak of Pat in the same way they speak of – toxic waste.

It's not because he's spent the last 25 years slagging off Connacht football (though he has), it all goes back to his 'performance' in the 1980 All-Ireland. After 11 minutes into the game Roscommon had the great Kerry team on the run and were leading 1-2 to no score and really rolling. Eventually the ball finally gets into the Kerry forward line and it goes to Pat when one of the Roscommon backs brushes lightly against him and Pat went down like a bag of spuds. Now I don't want to say he was down a long time but the next morning I was talking to my neighbour Paddy Joe. The poor man's cow was calving shortly before the match and he couldn't leave for the game until his brand new Charlois bull calf was born. So as soon as the calf was out Paddy Joe jumped into his glamorous car – a Morris Minor – and turned on the car radio. He was just in Tyrellspass when the match started and was just passing Harry's in Kinnegad when Pat went down injured. As he drove on he was hearing how Pat was rolling to the right and rolling to the left. Just as he took his place in the Hogan Stand: Pat finally got up. Within seconds he was flying up and down the wing like a March hare and setting up the goal for Mike Sheehy that turned the match. Ever since then we say in Roscommon that the two worst things about Pat Spillane are – his face.

In Tyrone they call him 'Puke' but in Roscommon we call him 'Pepper' because he always gets up your nose. Mind you he did redeem himself somewhat in the eyes of Roscommon people in December 2006 when he selected our minors triumph over his beloved Kerry in the All-Ireland final replay as his highlight of the year. It is never too late to give up your prejudices.

In return for sharing his insights about football with me for the last few years I taught him a bit about music. I explained to him that Yoko Ono was a singer, using the term in its broadest sense. He thought it was Japanese for 'one egg please'. I also tried to educate him about a healthy diet. He thought sugar diabetes was a Welsh heavyweight boxer.

A Mother's Love

I felt though it was my duty for this book to provide readers with an objective assessment of Pat. The only problem is where would I get it from? I couldn't ask any one from Mayo. They all hate him there. I couldn't ask any one from Kildare. They all really hate him there. And I certainly couldn't ask any one from Ulster – they despise him there.

In the end Pat indirectly gave me the answer himself about the best objective assessment because as we all know Pat's most famous comments as an analyst were about his mother's arthritis and the Armagh full-back line. So I decided to ask my mother what she thought of Pat. She said: "Oh, Pat Spillane: 8 All-Ireland medals, 9 All-Stars, twice player of the year. He had everything you could possibly want in a footballer – except two things – talent and good looks."

Holding Out For A Hero

But seriously, getting to know Pat has been a very educational experience for me. People often say you should never meet your heroes. What I have learned though is that you should always meet your anti-hero because in the last years I have discovered there is a lot more to Pat than the crotchety character we see on television. Although we have different personalities and even more radically different views on Connacht football, we share a lot of biases, prejudices and tastes. One of our shared idiosyncrasies is a fondness for compiling lists. So I thought I would include the Top Ten Pat Spillane qualities. The problem is I could not think of ten, so I had to limit it to two! In inverse order they are:

2.

He is very decisive. I would go as far as to say he's the most decisive and emphatic person I've ever met. He never, ever has any doubts – he's usually wrong – but he never has any doubts.

1.

He is well able to laugh at himself. Some people would say that's probably a good thing, as there's so much to laugh at.

An Eddie Hobbs' Moment

Pat's passion for the game is still as strong today as in his playing days. I saw this at first hand watching him filling in a credit card application form. When it came to the question that asked: "What is your position in the company?" He answered: "Left half-forward."

Triumph And Tragedy

Pat has always had the gift of the gab. In August 2003

Kerry walking champion Gillian O'Sullivan's single-minded determination reaped a handsome dividend when she won a silver medal in the World Championships in Paris. However, she didn't perhaps get the credit she deserved because walking is not a glamorous sport. Most of the sporting headlines that day were created by Tyrone's demolition of Kerry in the All-Ireland Football semi-final. Spillane commented typically on a mixed day for the Kingdom: "We saw a great day for Kerry sport when Gillian O'Sullivan won a silver medal in the European Championships. Then that same afternoon we saw Kerry implode against Tyrone in the All-Ireland semi-final. It was like winning the Lotto and then immediately finding out that you had only 24 hours to live!"

A Modern Day Miracle

It is a little known fact but in Tyrone fans think of Spillane as a life-saver and a miracle-worker. One supporter was in a horrific car-crash. He was on a life-support machine for several weeks. All kinds of novenas were said and holy medals were placed on his forehead but to no avail. As he was a mad Gaelic football fan someone in a fit of desperation brought in a VCR beside his bed and stuck on a video of Spillane's highlights from *The Sunday Game*. As soon as he made his 'puke football' comments the comatose patient got up from his bed and switched off the video. As astonished doctors and nurses looked on, he said: "That f**king idiot was wrecking my head."

Testing Times

The RTE Sports Department decided that it should have a test for all its sport pundits. After the exam the supervisor, Bill O'Herlihy pulled Spillane over to his desk after a test and said, "Pat, I have a feeling that you have been cheating on your tests."

"What makes you think that?" Spillane asked him.

"Well," said Bill, "I was looking over your test and the first question was 'Who is the leader of Fine Gael?' Colm O'Rourke, who sat next to you, put Enda Kenny and so did you."

"Everyone knows that he is the leader of Fine Gael," Pat defended himself.

"Well, the next question was 'Who was Fine Gael Leader before Enda Kenny?' Colm put 'I don't know,' and you put 'Me neither'."

A Bridge Too Far

Pat has been known to put his foot in his mouth. On one of his first nights presenting In *The Sunday Game* in 2004, after Meath beat Wicklow, he asked Bernard Flynn how well would Meath cope with Mick O'Dwyer's Laois in the Leinster semi-final. The only problem was that Laois hadn't played Carlow at that stage! Yet another apology due to the Carlow people.

The Top Ten

Whatever people's feelings about him nobody can deny that Pat has added to the colour of Gaelic games. He has provided many a classic quote down through the years.

The following are my Top Ten Favourites:

Number 1

"I can hardly walk properly from all my injuries from football, but one day I'll be unlucky."

Number 2

"Páidí (O'Shea) didn't have a Plan B when things went wrong; we looked like we didn't have a Plan A."

SPILLANE ON KERRY'S CAPITULATION TO MEATH IN 2001

Number 3

"Statistics are like a bikini. What they reveal is suggestive, but what they conceal is vital."

Number 4

"My mother has arthritis but even she has more pace than the Armagh full-back line."

THE FAMOUS HALF-TIME COMMENT BEFORE ARMAGH TURNED THE TABLES ON KERRY IN THE 2002 ALL-IRELAND FINAL

Number 5

"You get more contact in an old time waltz at an old folk's home than in a National League final."

SPILLANE TALKS DOWN TYRONE'S CHANCES IN 2002

Number 6

"They [Cavan] have a forward line that couldn't punch holes in a paper bag."

Number 7

"The first half was even, the second half was even worse."

SPILLANE REFLECTS ON AN
ULSTER CHAMPIONSHIP CLASH

Number 8

"I look down the hall and I see before me Peter Canavan, one of the greatest Tyrone players of all time. They call Peter Canavan 'God' up here. They call me a boll*x. I have eight All-Ireland medals and Peter Canavan has none."

SPILLANE AT A FUNCTION IN TYRONE IN THE 1990S

Number 9

"I'm more likely to beat Kylie Minogue as rear of the year than Mayo is to win the All-Ireland."

Number 10

"People often say Meath are dogged, determined and stubborn – and that's only the nice things they say about them."

What Goes Around Comes Around

When the tables are turned and people give their verdict on him, of course Spillane, as the GAA's biggest villain, is often undone by his own villainy. In Armagh they still go on about his infamous comments at half-time in the 2002 All-Ireland Final, especially about his mother's arthritis. In retaliation they have a story about a conversation that they say took place between him and his mother, when he was eight.

"Mam! I think I've been selected for the school Gaelic team."

"That's good," replied his mother, "but why aren't you sure?"

"Well, it hasn't been announced officially, but I overheard the coach saying that if I were in the team I'd be a great drawback."

Arrested Development

A week after his 'puke football' comments two new jokes did the rounds in GAA clubs in Tyrone. In the first Spillane rushes into the TV studios to talk to Joe Brolly: "Joe, Joe, I've finished my jigsaw and it only took me three weeks."

"What's so exciting about that?" asked Brolly.

"The box says two to four years."

Another time Kevin McStay was wondering why Spillane spent so much time staring at his glass of orange juice. Apparently it was because it said 'concentrate' on the carton!

Playing Around

In Donegal he also attracts a hostile reaction. In local folklore Joe Brolly, Ger Loughnane and Pat Spillane assembled for a round of golf on Mother's Day. All three of them were quite surprised at having been able to escape from the family for the day, and so they compared notes on how they managed it.

Joe Brolly said, "I bought my wife a dozen red roses, and she was so surprised and touched that she let me go."

Ger Loughnane said, "I bought my wife a diamond ring, and she was so thrilled that she let me go."

Spillane said, "Last night I had a big feed of garlic. When I woke up this morning I rolled on top of my wife, breathed with gusto onto her face and asked, 'Golf course or intercourse?' She blinked and replied, 'I'll put your clubs in the car.'"

Medical Notes

I am reliably informed that the most popular joke going around Ulster involves Pat walking into a sperm donor bank and saying to the receptionist, "I'd like to donate some sperm."

She asked him: "Have you ever donated before?"

He replied: "Yes. You should have my details on your computer."

The receptionist said: "Oh yes. But I see you're going to need help. Shall I get a lap dancer for you?"

"Why do I need help?" he asked.

The receptionist replied: "Well, it said on your record that you're a useless wank*r."

The Truth Is Stranger Than Fiction

A one hundred percent true story: Spillane was the main speaker at a major function of a prominent club in Ulster. At the end of the night a spectator went up to the MC for the evening, Adrian Logan from UTV, and said, "'Twas shocking to hear all that filthy language here this evening. That kind of talk has no place in the GAA."

Adrian nodded and just to make conversation asked the man what he thought of Pat Spillane. Logan was surprised with his response, "I can't stand that f**k**g c**t. He only talks sh*t*."

Fan Mail

Not surprisingly Spillane has attracted the ire of a lot of people, often resulting in some deliciously wicked barbs. The following are just a sample selection of anti-Spillane sentiment.

My Top Twenty are:

Number 1

"The real problem with the foot and mouth epidemic Pat was that you didn't get it."

TED WALSH

Number 2

"Pat Spillane has turned his life around. He used to be depressed and miserable. Now he's miserable and depressed."

MEATH FAN

Number 3

"Pat Spillane speaks straight from the shoulder – at least I can detect no higher origin in anything he says."

KILDARE FAN

Number 4

"Pat Spillane is a self-made man who worships his creator."

CORK FAN

Number 5

"Lost. Grey male cat. Unfriendly. Answers to the name of Pat Spillane. Neutered."

NOTICE SPOTTED IN CASTLEBAR

Number 6

"I call Spillane 'The Funeral Director' because he is always miserable looking."

DONEGAL FAN

Number 7

"Pat Spillane has all the grace of a cow trying to play the bagpipes."

SLIGO FAN

Number 8

"Pat Spillane is living proof that arrogance is ignorance matured."

ROSCOMMON FAN

Number 9

"Pat Spillane has a great future behind him."

GALWAY FAN

Number 10

"When he moved to presenter of The Sunday Game *Spillane switched from chief gobsh*te to chief interrogator."*

LIAM HAYES

Number 11

"Remember the good old days when the only thing that annoyed you about television was poor reception. Now the reception is perfect but they sent us Pat Spillane to punish us instead."

CAVAN FAN

Number 12

"Poor Pat Spillane can't carry on,
His face is green and sickly,
His heartbeat's slow,
His pulse is low,
O' get a doctor quickly."

PADRAIC NEARY

Number 13

"We had a Pat Spillane anagram competition. Apparently
the best anagram is Pet Anal Lips."

VISITOR TO THE KILKENNY CAT LAUGHS FESTIVAL

Number 14

"Pat Spillane was unusual from birth because his mother
had morning sickness after he was born."

GALWAY FAN

Number 15

Q: Why does Pat Spillane open yoghurt pots while still in the supermarket?
A: Because the lid says 'Open Here'.
Q: Why is Pat Spillane an egotist?
A: He is usually me-deep in conversation.
Q. What's the difference between God and Pat Spillane?
A. God doesn't think he's Pat Spillane.

SLIGO FAN

Number 16

"Pat Spillane had the speed of a race-horse, the strength of a plough-horse and the brains of a rocking horse."

WICKLOW FAN

Number 17

"As he got so many predictions wrong this year I'm sending Spillane a copy of Murray Walker's book: Unless I'm Very Much Mistaken."

DONEGAL FAN

Number 18

"To say Spillane is cranky is like saying it sometimes rains in April."

LEITRIM FAN

Number 19

"Trying to make sense of his analysis is like juggling mud."

WEXFORD FAN

Number 20

"Pat Spillane makes the Hunchback of Notre Dame seem handsome."

KILDARE FAN

TWO

The Man from Clare

It is sometimes said that Ger Loughnane is hurling's answer to Jose Mourinho. That is rubbish. Given that Feakle's second most famous person, behind Biddy Early, was annoying officials and giving out about referees long before 'the Special One'; it is much more accurate to say that Jose, in his amazing monocoloured overcoat, is soccer's answer to Ger Loughnane.

Former Liverpool manager, Bill Shankly, said of his full-back, Tommy Smith, that he would raise an argument in a graveyard. With commendable honesty Loughnane says that the same comment could be made about himself.

Ger brings some of the qualities he showed as a player to his job as a coach. In the 1976 League Final replay Eddie Keher got a head injury and the blood was pumping out of him necessitating a long delay while he got attention. Loughnane, ever helpful and compassionate, went up to him and said, "Jaysus Keher would you ever get up and get on with it. Sure there's nothing wrong with you!"

Honesty And The Best Policy

From his earliest days Loughnane told it as it was. He reached four without giving up the habit of sucking his thumb, though his mother had tried everything from bribery to reasoning to painting it with lemon juice to discourage the habit. Finally she tried threats, warning her son that, "If you don't stop sucking your thumb, your stomach is going to blow up like a balloon." The next Sunday coming out from Mass he saw a pregnant woman and considered her gravely for a minute, then spoke to her saying, "Uh-oh . . . I know what you've been doing."

When Silence Is Not Golden

The only person who can make Loughnane speechless is his wife Mary. This trend began shortly after their marriage. When he returned from work one day she said: "I have great news for you. Pretty soon we're going to be three in this house instead of two." Loughnane started glowing with happiness and kissing his wife he said, "Oh darling, I'm the happiest man in the world."

"I'm glad that you feel that way because tomorrow morning my mother moves in with us," she replied.

All Creatures Great And Small

Loughnane is fiercely proud of his farming roots and still loves the land. As a result he has a gift with animals. One day he brought his dog to a junior football match in Shannon. The dog leapt on to the pitch and took part in the game, scoring two points for the home side. After the game everyone rushed to congratulate the owner but Loughnane was having none of it. "He's a terrible disappointment to me. I wanted him to be a hurler."

Wish You Were Here

My favourite story about Ger though is that after Clare won the All-Ireland in 1995 Loughnane went to the travel agent and said: "We've won the All-Ireland – our first victory in the All-Ireland final for 81 years. We've plenty of money raised, we can go anywhere in the world. I've only one stipulation. We need to go somewhere where nobody knows anything about hurling."

The travel agent replied: "Sir, you have two choices: Thailand or Tipperary."

The Strife Of Brian

Loughnane attracts strong opinions. In 2001 I worked with him on a modest publication about his life, which showcased his characteristic reserve and understatement. One of my most vivid memories from that fascinating experience was asking him to write a pen-picture of each of the players on his Clare team. A few weeks later he handed me five foolscap pages with notes on each player from one to fifteen. Those five pages would make very interesting reading for many people in Clare but are locked away deep in a vault in a bank in Geneva. What struck me was the one that stood out visually from all the others. Underneath Brian Lohan's name were just three words in block letters: *SIMPLY THE BEST*.

Four years later on a frosty February evening in Ennis I had the honour to meet Brian, the best full-back I have ever seen, and I asked him: "What was Loughnane like?" I was curious if he would reciprocate the compliment. He furrowed his brow for a moment and then he summed up his former manager with four immortal words: "Loughnane was a brute!"

Are We There Yet?

Loughnane is known for his capacity to talk. One evening in the difficult year of 1998 he and Tony Considine were driving home late from a training session in Saint

Flannans. As the road was very frosty Considine was being very careful to drive safely. After he drove about ten miles a Garda pulled Considine over and said: "Sir, do you realize your passenger fell out of the car five miles back?"

To which Considine replied: "Thank God, I thought I had gone deaf."

Raising The Banner

There are so many words Loughnane has generated down the years. The following are

The following are my personal favourites by the man himself:

"Dying is easy. Winning a Munster final is hard."

LOUGHNANE AFTER CLARE END 63 YEARS IN THE WILDERNESS IN 1995

"A Munster final is not a funeral, though both can be very sad affairs."

I felt sicker than a pilgrim in Lourdes."

LOUGHNANE ON 'THE COLIN LYNCH AFFAIR' IN 1998

"Even Mother Teresa wouldn't support us."
LOUGHNANE ON THE SAME SAGA

"I have to buy flowers for my wife. She asked me last night how is that Michael Lyster looks so much more older than me."

"We've got grounds which are state of the art and administration which is state of the Ark."
ANOTHER DIG AT THE MUNSTER COUNCIL

"As a Clare minor my first introduction was under the late Paddy 'Duggie' Duggan who gave a most amazing speech in the dressing room in Limerick. While whacking a hurley off a table and as his false teeth did three laps of his mouth he called on the team to kill and maim the opposition before saying an 'Our Father' and three 'Hail Mary's'"

21

"He had a photographic memory that was never developed."

LOUGHNANE ON A MUNSTER COUNCIL OFFICIAL IN 1998

"People say I am mad but I prefer to think of myself as open to unconventional thinking."

LOUGHNANE ON HIS UNORTHODOX SELECTION POLICY

"I am sorry if I caused offence by comparing the Munster Council to donkeys. I wish to unreseverdly apologize to the donkeys."

LOUGHNANE AFTER THE CONTROVERSIES OF 1998

"I'm not giving away any secrets like that to Tipperary. If I had my way, I wouldn't even tell them the time of the throw-in."

LOUGHNANE ON HIS CONTROVERSIAL SELECTION POLICY

X

"What does posterity need me for? Nothing. But what would I like said about me at my funeral? I'd like someone to say, 'Look! He's moving!'"

Payback

Loughnane attracts massive comment. Tipperary fans love to belittle his intellectual capabilities. One of the club websites in the county has a joke about him going back to his playing days with Clare. One evening he rang the team coach Fr Harry Bohan and sounding rather upset, he mumbled, "I don't think I'll be at training this evening. I am having trouble with this jigsaw puzzle and I'm not going anywhere until I solve it."

Fr Harry replied, "Well, what sort of jigsaw puzzle is it?"

Loughnane said, "It's got a picture of a tiger on the box but none of the pieces seem to fit together."

Fr Harry, rather annoyed by now said, "Okay, give me five minutes and I'll come over and see what I can do."

After a while, Fr Harry reached the Loughnane house and went into the kitchen where Ger was sitting at the table, shuffling the orange pieces and looking confused.

Fr Harry looked at him and immediately realised what had happened said, "Ger, for God's sake put the *Frosties* back in the box!"

Heaven Sent

Given that Loughnane has said so many nice things about Brian Cody you would imagine that the Kilkenny hurling community would say nice things about him in return. Not a bit of it. A club publication in the county also made jokes about his shortcomings in the brains department. To illustrate his deficiencies in this area they published the tale of an incident involving Loughnane, Einstein and Seamus Heaney going to Heaven. When they get to the gate Saint Peter is introducing an identity check. He begins with Einstein who proves his identity by demonstrating the theory of relativity. He is then welcomed into Heaven. Next is Seamus Heaney who proves himself by composing an incredible poem about the Gates of Heaven. Heaney is warmly welcomed into Heaven. Then Saint Peter turns to Loughnane and says: "Einstein and Seamus Heaney have demonstrated their identity very decisively. How are we to know that you are who you say you are?"

A blank look came over Loughnane's face and after a few minutes of thought he asked: "Who are Einstein and Seamus Heaney?"

Saint Peter beamed a beatific smile and said: "Well answered. You really are Ger Loughnane. Make yourself at home here in Heaven. You'll be glad to hear we have a dunce's corner prepared especially for you."

The Golden Days Are Over

When he became Galway coach in 2006 the Cats' fans told the story of the Clare hurling fan who was walking through the streets of Ennis when he saw a sale on at a video shop. When he stopped to look he saw a video called 'Clare Hurling: The Golden Years'. The guy entered the shop and asked how much the video cost. €300, he was told. The hurling fan replied, "What! I'm not paying 300 euros just for a video. The shop owner replied, "No don't be silly, the video is 5 euros, the Beta-Max video player is 295 euros."

Bless Me Father

Loughnane also has antagonised one or two high profile clergy in Clare. A lorry driver and a Tipperary fan were heading down the Ennis road when he saw a priest at the side of the road. Feeling it was his duty, he stopped to give the priest a lift. A short time later, he saw Loughnane on the side of the road and aimed his lorry at him. At the last second, he thought of the priest with him and realized he couldn't run over the Galway manager, so he swerved, but he heard a thump anyway. Looking back as he drove on, he didn't see anything. He began to apologize for his behaviour to the priest. "I'm sorry, Father. I barley missed that f**k . . . that fella at the side of the road."

But the priest said, "Don't worry, son. I got him with my door."

The People Have Spoken

Some the classic 'anti-Loughnane' comments include:

"Ger Loughnane is paranoid. He's the Woody Allen of hurling."

TIPP FAN

"There's only one head bigger than Ger Loughnane's and that's Birkenhead."

LIMERICK FAN

"He cost Irish industry €25 million because workers were talking about Ger Loughnane when they should have been doing their jobs!"

CLARE FAN AFTER THE FAMOUS LOUGHNANE INTERVIEW ON CLARE FM AT THE HEIGHT OF THE COLIN LYNCH CONTROVERSY

"It would be easier if he was trying to sell Eircom shares."

CLARE FAN ON CYRIL LYONS'S TASK SUCCEEDING LOUGHNANE AS CLARE MANAGER

"Any chance of an autograph? It's for the wife. She really hates you!"

TIPP FAN TO GER LOUGHNANE

"Ger Loughnane was fair; he treated us all the same during training - like dogs."

ANON CLARE PLAYER

"Ger Loughnane should be made Minister for the Environment given his contribution to gas emissions."

IVAN YATES

"In Cork at the very mention of Loughnane's name we all burst into song. Mind you the song we sing is 'The Langer'!"

CORK FAN

THREE

No Ordinary Joe

In the 1990s Derry football produced one of the great characters in the history of the game, Joe Brolly. The barrister has since gone on to become one of the most colourful analysts on RTE. Joe never really surrendered to managers and was never short of self-confidence. This did not always endear him to his managers. One of them was heard to say, "He's down there now letting people know how good he is playing."

He did things his way like blowing kisses to fans after he scored a goal. This caused one Derry fan to remark: "At the best of times Joe Brolly is objectionable but when he blows kisses he's highly objectionable."

Brolly wasn't always complimentary to his teammates. After a club game a disconsolate new recruit to the team said, "I've never played so badly before."

Brolly appeared surprised, "You mean you've played before?"

After a county game one of his colleagues said proudly, "That was the best game I ever played."

Brolly said to him sympathetically: "Never mind. You mightn't be as bad the next time."

Joe has left an indelible mark on the world of punditry:

"He [Geoffrey McConigle] has an arse like two bags of cement."

"I am as politically correct as a Nuremberg rally."

"You don't like to put a dampener on the whole thing on the first day, because every team sallies forth with great hopes in their breasts but realistically only four or five teams can win the All-Ireland this year."

BROLLY'S CHEERFUL INTRODUCTION TO THE 2007 CHAMPIONSHIP

"He [Kieran McDonald] looks like a Swedish maid."

"He [Conor Mortimer] would be better off spending more time practising his shooting and less in the hair-dressers."

"Why don't sharks attack Pat Spillane – Professional courtesy."

"I was Derry's worst ever hurler. The manager used to shout at me: 'Kick the f**king thing'."

"Cavan looked like ducks in thunder when they played Antrim."

"Several of those players out there today aren't even the cousin of a county footballer."

BROLLY ON CAVAN V DOWN 2007

Thrills And Spills

Joe Brolly has also gone head to head with Colm O'Rourke in a few memorable exchanges.

The Top Three might be:

Number 1

Brolly: "You'd have thought there was a fatwah out on me."
O'Rourke: "There is."

Number 2

O'Rourke: "Maybe they're [Armagh] trying to keep Laois waiting in the sun, a bit like Kerry last year."
Brolly: "Or maybe they're sitting in there with some custard creams."

Number 3

Brolly: "Armagh were like a German Panzer division, they just rolled over Donegal."
O'Rourke: "Armagh won't thank you, you shouldn't have mentioned Panzer divisions – they got wiped out."
Brolly: "But only when they ran out of oil, and there's a plentiful supply of that in South Armagh."

BROLLY HAS ALSO HAD SOME NICE EXCHANGES WITH MICHAEL LYSTER. ONE OF THE MOST MEMORABLE WAS:
Lyster: "Are Donegal's streamlined jerseys so opponents couldn't grab a hold of them?"
Brolly: "No, they're strictly for the girls, non-stick jerseys."

Window Of Opportunity

As a player but even more so as a pundit Joe has antagonised a lot of people. The most popular story in Tyrone is of the time that Brolly went into a shop that sells curtains. He told the pretty assistant that he would like to buy a pair of curtains in the Derry colours. The saleswoman showed her several patterns, but Brolly seemed to have a hard time choosing. Finally he made his selection. The saleswoman asked what size curtains he needed. Brolly replied, "15 inches."

"15 inches?????" asked the assistant. "That sounds very small, what room are they for?"

Brolly tells her that they aren't for a room, but they are for his computer. The surprised saleswoman replies, "But, Sir, computers do not have curtains!"

Brolly says, "Helllllooooooooooo . . . I've got Windows."

Clueless

In Mayo the most popular joke is of the time Brolly walks into an electrical shop and says to the sales lady, "I'd like to buy this TV".

The saleperson says: "I'm sorry we don't sell to stup . . . to intellectually challenged TV pundits."

The next day Brolly returns to the shop but this time in disguise. Again he approaches the same salesperson and says: "I'd like to buy this TV."

The sales person says: "Sorry we don't sell to TV pundits."

Brolly asks: "How did you know I am a TV pundit?"

"Well," says the salesperson, "this is a microwave."

Scientific Experiment

After yet another scathing Brolly attack on the shortcomings of the Kildare forward line a man was heard to ask in a barber's shop, "What do you get if you cross Joe Brolly with a chewing gum?"

"Dumb and gummer!!"

Pat Spillane and Joe Brolly walk into a building. You'd think one of them would have seen it.

Doctor, Doctor

In Roscommon they tell the story of the day Brolly went to the doctor and told her that his body hurt wherever he touched it. "Impossible," says the Doctor, "show me."

He takes his finger and pushes his elbow and screams in agony. He pushes his knee and screams, pushes his ankle and screams.

"I thought so," the Doctor says. "Your finger is broken."

So This Is Christmas

The Santa Claus at the shopping centre was very surprised when a young lady about 20 years old walked up and sat on his lap. Santa didn't usually take requests from adults, but she smiled very nicely at him, so he asked her, "What do you want for Christmas?"

"Something for my father please," said the young lady.

"Something for your father? Well, that's very thoughtful of you," smiled Santa. "What do you want me to bring him?"

Without blinking, she replied, "A one-way ticket to the North Pole for Joe Brolly."

Fair Fight

Pat Spillane describes how one night he was walking out of the RTE studios and he saw Joe Brolly and one of his friends were being assaulted by a group of Tyrone fans after Brolly had made yet another incidenary attack on the Tyrone team. He yelled out: "Spillane could you give me and my friend some help."

Spillane coolly replied: "I'm always glad to help. You don't say: 'Me and my friend.' You say: 'My friend and I'." Then he got into his car and drove off.

Legal Eagles

Armagh star turned pundit Jarlath Burns enjoys a joke about lawyers at Brolly's expense.

An engineer dies and reports to hell. Pretty soon, the engineer gets dissatisfied with the level of comfort in hell, and starts designing and building improvements. After a while, they've got air conditioning and flush toilets and escalators, and the engineer becomes hugely popular. One day God calls the devil up on the telephone and says with a sneer, "So, how's it going down there in hell?"

The devil replies, "Things are going great. We've got air conditioning and flush toilets and escalators, and who knows what this engineer will come up with next."

God replies, "What??? You've got an engineer? That's a mistake – he should never have gotten down there; send him up here."

The devil says, "No way. I like having an engineer on the staff, and I'm keeping him."

God says, "Send him back up here or I'll get Joe Brolly and sue."

Satan laughs uproariously and replies, "Yeah, sure. And just where are you going to get a lawyer?"

Unforgettable Fire

A Donegal fan tells the story about three GAA pundits who are to be executed. Kevin McStay is brought forward first, and the executioner asks if he has any last requests. He says no, and the executioner shouts, "Ready . . . Aim . . ."

Suddenly McStay yells, "Earthquake". Everyone is startled and looks around. He manages to escape.

The angry guard then brings Anthony Tohill forward, and the executioner asks if he has any last requests, He says "No", and the executioner shouts, "Ready . . . Aim.."

Tohill then screams, "Tornado". Yet again, everyone is startled and looks around. He too escapes execution. By this point, Joe Brolly had figured out what the others are doing. The guards bring him forward, and the executioner asks if he has any last requests. He also says "No", and the executioner shouts, "Ready . . . Aim . . ."
Brolly shouts, "Fire."

Backchat

Actions have consequences. Brolly has also been the victim of some great one-liners:

"Didn't you used to be Pat Spillane?"
CONFUSED DONEGAL FAN
"The reason why I object to Ulster football is that has it inflicted Joe Brolly on us!"
PAT SPILLANE

"You're no ordinary Joe."
TOMMY LYONS

"What would finally help drag Brolly into the Premier League of GAA analysts is a copy of the 'How to be as good an analyst as Colm O'Rourke self-help book' *but it hasn't been written yet."*

MEATH FAN

"Joe Brolly is proof of the tendency of stupid ideas to seem smarter when they come at you rapidly."

FERMANAGH FAN

"Brolly talks like Speedy Gonzalez on a caffeine high."

ARMAGH FAN

"If they wrote a book about the nice things we say about Joe Brolly it would be shorter than the Amish phone directory."

TYRONE FAN

"When two egotists like Brolly and Spillane meet, it's an I for an I."

DISGRUNTLED LEITRIM FAN

"Brolly you wouldn't get a kick in a stampede."

TYRONE FAN TO BROLLY ON A TRAIN

FOUR

Managerspeak

Tempora mutantur nos et mutamur in illis: Times change and we change with them. One of the biggest changes in the world of the GAA over the last 30 years has been the prominence of the manager. It began in the 1970s with Kevin Heffernan and Mick O'Dwyer. Some people though wonder if there is mercenary reason behind all this and recount the story of the rich GAA manager, the poor GAA manager and the tooth fairy who are in a room with a €100 note on the table when the lights go out. When the light comes back on: the money is gone. So who took it? It's got to be the rich GAA manager because the other two are figments of the imagination.

The Big Question

In 1990 Nelson Mandela was freed from his years in captivity. The first thing he allegedly said after he was released was: "Have Wicklow won a Championship match since I was thrown into that bloody place?" Having been in the doldrums for so long the appointment of Mick O'Dwyer in late 2006 was designed to change all that.

Time To Say Goodbye

After O'Dwyer retired as Kildare manager he subsequently met his successor, Padraig Nolan. He wished Nolan the best of luck and ushered him aside, "Just a little advice, as tradition goes from one outgoing Kildare manager to the next, take these."

He handed him three envelopes. "If you fail to lead Kildare to victory," Dwyer said, "open an envelope, and inside you will find some invaluable advice as to how to proceed."

Nolan got off to a flyer and Kildare had a string of victories in the O'Byrne Cup. Then when Kildare began their National League campaign things started to go badly wrong. Nolan remembered O'Dwyer's envelopes and after a bad defeat he opened the first envelope. "Blame the referee," it said.

He walked confidently into the informal press conference and said, "Well, there wasn't much between the teams really. In a match like that small mistakes can change the complexion of the game completely and in that respect I felt that the ref made some decisions that went against us which had a big bearing on the final outcome."

The journalists nodded wisely. O'Dwyer's advice was working well.

Another defeat quickly followed. Bad news; Nolan would have to use the second of the three envelopes.

"Blame the free-taker," it said. Off Nolan went to face the media.

"Well. I thought it was nip and tuck, we had them under pressure, but unfortunately we tried a few different lads taking our frees, but unfortunately we didn't have the best of days with the old shooting boots and so the chances slipped away."

Again the journalists seemed satisfied with his response. Thank God for these get-out-of-jail-free envelopes Nolan reflected, though he still had failed to take Kildare forward and he knew that he was storing up trouble for himself.

One of the few bright spots in Kildare's 2003 League campaign had been a win over Sligo – the team that had won the hearts of the nation the previous year with their gutsy performances in the Championship (inspired by the wonderful Eamon O'Hara) and that had pushed Armagh the hardest of all their opponents in their historic Sam Maguire triumph. However, Kildare had broken a technical rule in the game and had the points taken off them. As a result they had to play off against Sligo on Easter Sunday to see who would be relegated. Ten thousand people attended the game. Serious pressure. Kildare began brightly and appeared to be in the ascendancy but had two players sent off. Sligo went on to claim victory. Nolan was heartbroken not to have won. There was only one consolation: help was at hand. He walked into the dressing-room, looking forward to some first class advice from the third and last white envelope. He rummaged in his bag, pulled it out and tore it open. The advice was simple, "Start writing out three new envelopes."

Food For Thought

Mikey Sheehy rings Mick O'Dwyer and tells him that he's just been invited by his old school to tell him all that he knew about football. He asked O'Dwyer what he should say.

Dwyer replied: "Tell them you've got flu."

Bon Appetit

My favourite O'Dwyer story though relates to the fact that every day he goes to a pub in Listowel for lunch and always orders the soup of the day. One day the Manager asks him how he likes his meal. O'Dwyer replies, "Twas good, but you could give a little more bread."

So the next day the Manager tells the waitress to give him four slices of bread. The Manager asks him afterwards how he liked his meal. O'Dwyer replies, "Twas good, but you could give a little more bread."

So the next day the Manager tells the waitress to give him eight slices of bread. "How was your meal today, sir?" the Manager asks. O'Dwyer replies, "Twas good, but you could give a little more bread."

The following day the Manager tells the waitress to give him a whole loaf of bread with his soup. "How was your meal, sir?" the Manager asks, when he comes to pay.

O'Dwyer replies, "Twas good, but you could give a little more bread."

The Manager is now obsessed with seeing his famous customer say that he is satisfied with his meal, so he goes to the bakery, and orders a six-foot-long loaf of bread. When O'Dwyer comes in as usual the next day, the waitress and the Manager cut the loaf in half, butter the entire length of each half, and lay it out along the counter, right next to his bowl of soup. O'Dwyer sits down, and devours both his bowl of soup, and both halves of the six-foot-long loaf of bread.

The Manager now thinks he will get the answer he is looking for, and when O'Dwyer comes up to pay for his meal, the Manager asks in his usual way: "How was your meal TODAY, sir?"

O'Dwyer replies: "It was good as usual, but I see you've gone back to giving only two slices of bread."

The Lyons Den

As Dublin Manager Tommy Lyons was not known to mince his words. Once when he brought the Dublin team for a bonding weekend in a hotel, he called over the head waiter the second morning. "Good morning, sir! I'd like to order two boiled eggs, one of them so undercooked that it's runny, and the other so overcooked that it's tough. I also want some rubbery bacon, burnt toast, and butter that's so cold it's impossible to spread. Finally, I'll have a pot of extra-weak coffee, served at room temperature." The bewildered waiter almost stuttered. "Sir! We cannot serve such an awful breakfast to you here."

"Why not?" Lyons replied. "That's what I got here yesterday."

Money, Money, Money

Tommy Lyons has been known to poke gentle fun at colleagues. One of his occasional targets is Mick O'Dwyer, in particular his reputation for being 'careful with money'. A story attributed to Lyons relates to the time John O'Mahony brings in the Mayo team into a pub and orders pints for each of them. The barman says to him the pint only cost five cents each. O'Mahony is amazed and asks the barman, "Why so cheap?" The barman replies that because it was exactly 100 years that day since the pub was opened they were selling drinks at what they cost 100 years ago. O'Mahony notices Mick O'Dwyer and the Wicklow team standing in the corner not buying drinks. O'Mahony asks the barman what is the story. The barman replies: "Oh, Mick O'Dwyer's waiting for happy hour."

Low Maintenance

Another story in that context is about the day O'Dwyer was riding in the back of his limousine when he saw two men eating grass by the road side. He ordered his driver to stop and he got out to investigate.

"Why are you eating grass?" he asks one man.

"We don't have any money for food," the poor man replies.

"Oh, come along with me then," instructs O'Dwyer.

"But, sir, I have a wife and two children!"

"Bring them along!" replies Mick. He turns to the other man and says, "Come with us."

"But sir, I have a wife and six children," the second man answers.

"Bring them as well!" replies O'Dwyer as he heads for the limo.

They all climb into the car, which is no easy task, even for a car as large as the limo. Once underway, one of the poor men says, "Sir, you are too kind. Thank you for taking all of us with you."

O'Dwyer replies, "No problem, the grass at my home is almost a foot tall."

The Doors

Despite his friendship with Pat Spillane Lyons is also known for his tendency to tell stories against Kerry's most famous pundit. When the Kerry team were on tour in Australia in the 1980s Mick O'Dwyer noticed that Spillane was missing when the team assembled in the hotel foyer. He knew which room his number twelve was in at the hotel and called him up wondering what happened to him. Spillane told him he couldn't get out of his room.

"You can't get out of your room?" O'Dwyer asked, "Why not?"

Spillane replied, "There are only three doors in here. One is the bathroom, one is the closet, and one has a sign on it that says 'Do not disturb!'."

Lost

Lyons was left eating humble pie when Westmeath shocked the Dubs in the 2004 Leinster Championship. Everyone was gunning for him. He did get an unexpected phone call later that evening from the world's leading film-maker, Stephen Spielberg. Having heard about Ciaran Whelan's performance in the match he wanted to cast him in his next film, *The Invisible Man*.

After the game the story doing the rounds in Meath was that Lyons rings Mickey Harte after Tyrone winning the 2003 All-Ireland and asks what's the recipe for winning an All-Ireland final? Harte says you get the following drill: "Get loads of cones, placing them carefully around the field; loads of balls; have the players soloing around the cones, doing one-twos, side-steps, swerves, and kicking the ball over the bar."

After a few weeks Harte was surprised that Lyons hadn't rang him to thank him for his brilliant advice, so he rang Lyons and asked him how well they'd get on.

"Not great. The cones beat us by six points."

Danger

After losing to Westmeath Tommy did take remedial reaction afterwards; like recalling Dessie Farrell to the Dublin panel. I enjoyed Dessie's comments about one of his teammates: "The opposition are much more dangerous when he has the ball."

The Times They Are A Changing

Management today is very different from when John O'Mahony started off in the 1980s. When he took over as Mayo boss for the second time in 2006 he asked three of his players what their grandchildren would be saying about them.

I would like my grandchildren to say, "He was successful in business," declared James Nallen.

"Fifty years from now," said Kieran MacDonald, "I want them to say, 'He was a loyal family man'."

Turning to Conor Mortimer, O'Mahony asked, "So what do you want them to say about you in 50 years?"

"Me?" Mortimer replied. "I want them all to say, 'He certainly looks good for the age'!"

The 10 Winning Comments

Despite his caution talking up his team in the media John O'Mahony has produced some nice lines down the years.

My Top Ten are:

Number 1

"Whenever a team loses there's always a row at half-time but when they win it's an inspirational speech."

Number 2

"There is more politics in the GAA than in the United Nations."

Number 3

"The difference between ordinary and extraordinary is a little extra."

Number 4

"The theories we believe: we call facts, and the facts we disbelieve: we call theories."

Number 5

"Take the opportunity of a lifetime during the lifetime of the opportunity."

Number 6

"The only time you are aware that you have a big reputation is when you fail to live up to it."

Number 7

"A coach is like a winemaker: he must produce the best wine with the grapes available."

Number 8

"The only place where succeess comes before work is in the dictionary."

Number 9

"Being in the right does not depend on having a loud voice."

Number 10

"Good ball is when we have it. Bad ball is when the other side have it."

Born To Run

Managers have brought a number of new trends with them. Fitness gurus are all the rage. When the iron man from Rhode Paddy McCormack was training Offaly for a year his style of training was laps, laps and more laps. Eventually the players said to him: "We're sick to the death of all those laps. Tonight we're going to have something different." Paddy thought for a moment and said: "Okay lads that's fine. Turn around the other way for a change."

Love And Hate

Managers are loved and hated in equal measure. Doctor Pat O'Neill trained Dublin to the All-Ireland Final in 1995. He was known for his extraordinary treatment of arthritis. One day he had a waiting room full of people when a little old lady, bent over almost in half, shuffled in slowly, leaning on her cane. When her turn came, she went into the doctor's office. Within five minutes she came back out walking completely erect. A woman in the waiting room who had seen all this rushed up to the little old lady and said, "It's a miracle! You walked in bent in half, and now you're walking erect. What did the doctor do?"

"Gave me a longer cane," the woman replied.

Former Donegal manager Brian McEniff runs a very successful hotel business. One day he went over to say hello to a group of women out to lunch in his hotel to celebrate the birthday of their oldest friend. One of the ladies said, "This is a very special occasion. It's Paula's ninety-fifth birthday." Brian made several enemies and one friend for life when he asked, "Which one of you is Paula?"

When Mickey Drove Joe

One man who understands the pressure managers are under is the 2007 Open winner Padraig Harrington; a great Gaelic games fan. No managers would share one of his mantras: 'I want to focus on my focus' more than Mickey Harte and Joe Kernan. The two men are always looking for any stroke to put their opponent under pressure. Both were driving up to Dublin together for a promotional event a few days before their teams met in the Ulster Championship. Harte was driving but hates wearing a seat belt and went into a panic when he saw a Garda pulling them over. He says to Big Joe, "Quick, take the wheel. I gotta put my seat belt on."

So he did that as the Garda approached. The Garda knocked on the window and said: "Say, I noticed you weren't wearing your seat belt."

Harte said, "I was, but you don't have to take my word for it – this man here is a good Christian man, ask him; he'll tell you the truth. He doesn't lie about anything." The Garda says to Big Joe, "So? How about it, sir?"

And Kernan said: "I've known this man for 20 years, Guard, and one thing I've learned in all that time is – you never argue with him when he's drunk."

Riddle Me This

Sometimes managers' efforts to be innovative cause confusion. Paul 'Pillar' Caffrey caused some raised eyebrows amongst his Dublin squad when he asked: "What is the best way to communicate with a fish?"

They all scratched their heads but nobody could come up with the answer: "Drop it a line."

Mind Your Language

In a former life Roscommon and former Clare, Mayo, Fermanagh and again Mayo manager, John Maughan, was an army officer. One day he was trying to teach a bunch of raw recruits how to handle the rifle. The rookies were firing hither and yon and one of them shot Maughan in the seat of his pants. "You *******, ****. You worthless piece of ****," screamed Maughan.

A fellow officer immediately reminded the badly bleeding Maughan of the army's anti-bullying code. Maughan immediately composed himself and turned back to the recruit. "My goodness, gracious," he said, "what on earth was your motivation in shooting me with an unwarranted expenditure of valuable ammunition?"

Mixed Bag

There are no limits to the unusual situations managers find themselves confronted with as the following selection of heartfelt observations reveal:

"Hurry up and make a decision ref. I have to go home to bale the hay!"

THE LATE MICHAEL YOUNG DURING A CLUB GAME IN DERRY AS THE REF DITHERED ABOUT WHETHER TO AWARD A PENALTY

Anxious corner-forward before club match in Sligo: "Do you think I need gloves?"
Mentor: "For all the ball you'll get, it's not going to matter."

"We're taking you off but we're not bothering to put on a sub. Just having you off will improve our situation!"

MENTOR TO CLUB PLAYER IN DERRY

Eugene McGee: "Well what happened?"
Offaly player late for training: "Oh, the wheel fell off my mobile home."

McGEE ONCE THREATENED HIS SQUAD THAT HE WOULD WRITE A BOOK OF OFFALY EXCUSES

Mick Holden (seriously late for training on a Saturday morning): "I was coming across town and I was stopped by the guards. They said I was a match for one of the guys that pulled that big bank robbery yesterday."
Kevin Heffernan: "Really?"
Holden: "No, but it sounds so much better than saying I slept it out."

Kevin Heffernan handing out sleeping tablets before an All-Ireland final to volunteers: "I never thought you'd have any problems sleeping."
Mick Holden: "Oh these are not for me. I sleep like a baby. These are for my mother. She can never sleep the night before a big match!"

"I warned the boys they couldn't go through the league unbeaten, and, unfortunately, they appear to have listened to me!"
TYRONE ART MCRORY AFTER HIS SIDE'S DEFEAT BY DONEGAL

"Kieran Donaghys don't grow on trees."
LIAM KEARNS

Derry mentor: "Seamus you're coming off."
Seamus: "But we have only the bare 15."
Mentor: "For the sake of the team you're coming off anyway."

"The most important skill for any manager these days is to have a good excuse."

TOMMY LYONS

"I didn't know what was going on at the start in the swirling wind. The flags were all going in different directions and I thought they must have starched them to fool us."

MICK O'DWYER

Fr Mick at the club's AGM: "It's not the winning but the taking part that counts."
Club Manager Sean 'The Straight Talker' Smith: "Father, that's the kind of sh**te talk that sickens my hole."

"Come on now lads. Let's go out there and show them up. It's plain to be seen. They can't score points!"

THE MANAGER-CUM-TRAINER-CUM-CLUB SECRETARY-CUM GROUNDSKEEPER OF A CLUB TEAM FROM LEITRIM WHO TRAVELLED 200 MILES TO A TOURNAMENT GAME IN WATERFORD GIVING HIS HALF-TIME PEP TALK. THEY TRAILED BY 7-2 TO 0-5

"Mick, would you ever mind my false teeth."

CAVAN'S JIM O'DONNELL STROLLING OVER TO THE SIDELINE IN
THE MIDDLE OF A MATCH AGAINST ARMAGH TO HAND HIS
MOLARS TO MANAGER, MICK HIGGINS

Unfair On The Fair City?

Meath are good for the game, if for no reason other than their rivalry with the Dubs. Dublin have been waiting for the Sam Maguire Cup for a long time. In Meath they tell the story that in the middle of the night the then Dublin County Chairman, John Bailey, was woken up by a call from his local Garda Station. "I'm afraid the trophy room has been broken into, sir." Horrified, Bailey asked, "Did they get the cups?" "No, sir," replied the Garda, "they didn't go into the kitchen." Rumour had it they were sued by the burglars for wasting their time.

The Fab Four

The traditional rivalry between Dublin and Meath has added so much to Gaelic games, particularly in the four epic contests in 1991. This was no place for the faint-hearted. A GAA referee died and went to heaven after ruling out a goal from a star player; not giving a penalty when the player was grounded and giving a very dubious looking goal to the other team. Stopped by St Peter at the gates, he was told that only brave people who had performed heroic deeds and had the courage of their convictions could enter. If the ref could describe a situation in his life where he had shown all these characteristics, he would be allowed in. "Well," said the ref, "I was reffing a game between Dublin and Meath at Croke Park. Meath were ahead, with seconds left in the match. A Dublin forward made a break and weaved through the Meath defence and scored a goal. However, he took too many steps, but as Dublin were clearly the better side, I ruled that he scored a legitimate goal."

"My word, that was indeed brave of you, but I will have to check the facts in the celestial book," said St Peter, and departed to look it up. He returned with a puzzled look and said, "Sorry, but there is no record of this. Can you help me to trace it? When did it happen?"

The ref looked at his watch and replied, "About 45 seconds ago!"

Boiling Boylan

For an entire generation memories of Meath-Dublin clashes are linked inextricably to Sean Boylan. He is the exception that proves the rule – every rule of management! A lovely man, yet he has an inner steel to him. In 1987 he sensationally resigned as Meath Manager because he felt that the team needed to make a bigger effort in training. The players asked Joe Cassells to ring him and persuade him to return. The call was made and a change of heart ensued. At the first training session afterwards Boylan said, "I believe I owe you ten pence for the phone call."

To riotous laughter from the Meath squad Cassells replied, "Nah, it's okay, I reversed the charges."

Tactical Confusion

Sean Boylan has always been willing to let players know that their best days are behind them and carried out radical surgery on a successful team. A former Meath player of some note was speaking to Boylan about tactics after giving a less than distinguished performance in a challenge match. The player shrugged his shoulders and said, "I'm confused, I don't know whether I'm coming or going."

Boylan put his arm on his shoulder, looked him straight in the eye and whispered softly: "I'm afraid, X, you're going."

Fear Crua

This year one of Boylan's protégées, Colm Coyle, took Sean's place on the Meath sideline – or at least he did when he was not suspended. As a teak-tough defender Coyle embodied the stereotype of tough, hard Meath players and as a result had the odd problem with referees! I enjoyed Colm's reaction after the Monaghan team he managed a few years ago beat Armagh: "We planned for every eventuality, including if we had a man sent off. I told them what Meath did every time I was sent off!"

Cool Hand Luke

When Luke Dempsey moved to manage Longford after earning a fine reputation with Westmeath it was a significant readjustment for him. One of the stories told about him from his first match in charge arose when one of his forwards had just suffered a severe blow in the region of his essential equipment. Luke ran onto the field with his first-aid gear and as he approached, the injured player was squirming on the ground with his hands clutched between his legs, moaning, "Please, don't rub 'em. Just count 'em!"

Another story goes back to his first game in charge of Westmeath when he burst into the changing room as the second half of the game was about to begin.

"All right!" he roared. "All of you lazy, no-good, thick-headed b*stards – out on that field – now!" All the players jumped to their feet and rushed onto the field – except for Dessie Dolan sitting in the corner. "Well!" roared Luke.

"Well," said Dessie, "There certainly were a lot of them, weren't there."

Unlovely Leitrim

After a training session one evening a number of years ago a Leitrim manager, who shall remain nameless, was surprised to receive a call from the County Chairman. He was even more surprised when the Chairman asked him if he'd ever thought about retirement. "Good heavens, no," said the Manager.

"Well, I should if I were you," said the Chairman. "I have to tell you that you're fired."

Mean Martin

After leading Cavan to an Ulster championship Martin McHugh's popularity waned significantly in bitter rivals Monaghan. Some of their fans started telling stories about Martin. In one he was standing in front of a soda machine outside the local Centra. After putting in a euro, a can of *Cidona* popped out of the machine. McHugh placed it on the ground, put another euro into the machine, and pushed another button; suddenly a can of coke come out of the machine. He continued to do this until a woman waiting to use the machine became impatient. "Excuse me, can I get my soda and then you can go back to whatever stupid thing you are doing?"

Martin is supposed to have turned around and said, "Yeah right! I'm not giving up the machine while I'm still winning."

Another is about the day Martin went playing golf with

Colm O'Rourke. After the game he raced off leaving Colm to tip the two caddies. When they met up later Martin asked Colm if he had tipped the caddies. He replied: "Yes. I gave my caddy 30 euros and yours; 30 cents on your behalf."

Martin blurted out: "30 cents. Sure you might as well have given him nothing."

O'Rourke gave McHugh that dismissive look he normally reserves for Joe Brolly and said: "If I gave him nothing he would have thought you forgot. By giving him 30 cents he now knows what the whole country knows – that you are a mean ba*tard."

Talkback

Managers down through the years have produced more than the odd *bon mot*:

"We had to work very hard for this – it took 119 years for us to get it."

TYRONE BOSS MICKEY HARTE AFTER WINNING THE 2003 ALL-IRELAND

"Did you ever hear 'One day at a time, sweet Jesus?' Before yesterday there were no All-Irelands in Tyrone, now there's one."

MICKEY HARTE WHEN ASKED ABOUT THE POSSIBILITY OF TWO-IN-A-ROW

"A late tackle in Monaghan is one that comes the day after the match!"

EUGENE MCGEE

"Hello Jack Lynch, you were great to come."

JIM HURLEY, CHAIRMAN OF THE CORK SELECTION COMMITTEE, WHEN LYNCH SHOWED UP IN CROKE PARK WITH ONLY ABOUT 15 MINUTES BEFORE THE THROW-IN IN THE 1945 ALL-IRELAND FOOTBALL FINAL

"You should be used to being close to vegetables where you work!"

REMARK ATTRIBUTED TO THE CURRENT PRO OF THE GAA DANNY LYNCH IN HIS PRE-CROKE PARK INCARNATION WHEN HE WORKED FOR THE OPW. HE WENT TO VISIT LIAM MULVHILL IN HOSPITAL. MULVHILL HAD BEEN IN A CAR ACCIDENT – WITH HIS CAR GOING THROUGH A HEDGE INTO A VEGETABLE FIELD

"While there are many claims that managers are being paid under the table; the GAA couldn't even find the tables!"

FORMER GAA PRESIDENT PETER QUINN

"Ah sure, we're all going around with our arse out of our trousers."

MICK O'DWYER ON RUMOURS THAT GAA MANAGERS ARE
BEING PAID MONEY UNDER THE TABLE

"When I played we got a piece of orange at halftime, and if you were very quick you might get two."

MICK O'DWYER

"Managing a county team means commitment. Of course, so does insanity."

SEÁN BOYLAN

FIVE

Hurlers on the Ditch

For a long time football managers enjoyed a higher media profile than their hurling counterparts. All this was to change with the arrival of one of hurling's great evangelists, Liam Griffin, as Wexford Manager. Of course hurling fans will never forget the way he steered Wexford to that All-Ireland in 1996. After he took over the team he did a bonding exercise with them. One of his questions was: "What is your favourite position?" Most players answered in the obvious way, "full-back, centre half-back, full-forward" etc. The exception was a new panellist to *The Sunday Game* in 2004, the joker from Faythe Harriers, Larry O'Gorman, who gave Griffin information he didn't really need. His reply was simply, "On Top!"

Griffin was a man who planned for all eventualities. A case in point came before the 1996 All-Ireland Hurling Final when he announced to the panel: "We have a plan if a man gets sent off."

Tom Dempsey immediately piped up: "So you're going to manage two teams."

When he stepped down as Wexford manager it was inevitable that his services as an analyst would be in great demand and RTE audiences have had the benefit of his passion for "the Riverdance of sport". With his knowledge of the game he quickly became the Alan Hansen of co-commentary. In a world where words are cheap the only pity is that Liam's sharp intelligence and clear elucidation could not be deployed by cross-channel stations for their soccer half-time discussions. Often the brightest thing about their analysis is Terry Venables's jacket.

Alone All Alone

Another of the big personalities in hurling management is former Tipperary boss Babs Keating. He once faced the problem of rallying his team even though they were trailing at half-time by eight points. After a number of inspirational words in an effort to instil confidence Babs went around the team individually and asked each of them: "Can we do it?"

To the man they replied: "We can. We can."

He could feel the surge of belief invading the dressing-room. Everything was going swimmingly until he turned to Joe Hayes and asked: "Joe, can we do it?"

Joe took the wind out of his sails when he replied: "It's not looking good."

After Tipperary crashed out of the Championship in 2006 Babs was subjected to gentle criticism. His fall from grace is reflected in the comment of one former Tipperary player who is not in the Babs' fan club, "The only way Babs can get up again is with Viagra."

Babs Talk

With the obvious exception of Ger Loughnane few hurling managers have inspired as many quotes as Babs Keating.

Some of those that can be published include:

"The miracle of Babs [Keating] is his tongue."
TOM HUMPHRIES

"You can be expelled from the NUJ if you are within half a mile of Babs when he speaks and you don't record it."

TOM HUMPHRIES

"Babs loves microphones. If he could grow them in his garden he'd be out there all the time talking to them like Prince Charles to his daffodils."

TOM HUMPHRIES

"If Babs Keating wrote a book on humility he'd be raging if it wasn't displayed in the shop window."

OFFALY FAN IN 1998

"Babs Keating 'resigned' as coach because of illness and fatigue. The players were sick and tired of him."

OFFALY FAN IN 1998

"Babs Keating has about as much personality as a tennis racket."

OFFALY FAN IN 1998

"Babs Keating has been arrested in Nenagh for shaking a cigarette machine, but the Gardaí let him off when he said he only wanted to borrow 20 players."

WATERFORD FAN AFTER BABS HAD PREDICTED A HEAVY DEFEAT FOR WATERFORD IN THE 2002 MUNSTER FINAL

"Babs Keating said to me one night that the difference between a pat on the back and a kick in the arse is a foot and a half."

BRIAN KERR (UNDER PRESSURE)

BABS HIMSELF HAS PRODUCED CLASSIC QUOTES LIKE:

"You can't win derbies with donkeys."

BABS BEFORE TIPPERARY PLAYED CORK IN THE 1990 MUNSTER FINAL. THE CORK DONKEYS WON

"Sheep in a heap."

BABS' DESCRIPTION OF THE OFFALY HURLERS IN 1998

"There's some fool texting me during matches – I hope he loses his phone for the rest of his life."

BABS AFTER TIPP SHOCKED CORK IN 2007

"I was the first hurling manager to be forced to retire due to public demand."

BABS ON RESIGNING AS OFFALY MANAGER IN 1998

Get Smart

One Tipperary All-Ireland winning player is known for his keen intelligence. This trait was evident from an early age if a story heard in Nenagh is to be believed. When he was a young man he entered the confessional box and said, "Bless me, Father, for I have sinned. I have been with a loose woman."

The priest asked, "And who was the woman you were with?"

"Sure and I can't be telling you, Father. I don't want to ruin her reputation."

"Well I'm sure to find out sooner or later, so you may as well tell me now. Was it Mary?"

"I cannot say."

"Was it Monica?"

"I'll never tell."

"Was it Lizzie?"

"I'm sorry, but I'll not name her."

"Was it Patsy?"

"My lips are sealed."

"Was it Fiona, then?"

"Please, Father, I cannot tell you."

The priest sighs in frustration.

"You're a steadfast lad, and I admire that. But you've sinned, and you must atone. Be off with you now."

The player walked back to his pew. His friend slid over and whispers, "What did you get?"

"Five good leads," said the Tipperary star.

Straight Talk

Cork hurling manager Gerald McCarthy is not a man to mince his words. This was apparent at an early age. His mother invited some people to dinner. At the table, she turned to six-year-old Gerald and said, "Would you like to say the blessing?"

"I wouldn't know what to say," Gerald replied.

"Just say what you hear Mommy say," his mother said.

Little Gerald bowed his head and said, "Dear Lord, why on earth did I invite all these people to dinner?"

The Three Wise Men

The night before the 1966 All-Ireland Final the three Macs: Charlie, Justin and Gerald McCarthy were supposed to be tucked up in their beds for a night. The three young men decided to take a trip into the city centre to sample the atmosphere. The problem was that it was much harder for them to get a taxi back to the team hotel than they expected. Two of the team mentors Jim 'Tough' Barry and Donie Keane were patrolling the corridor. The three lads knew they would be read the riot act so they hid until the coast was clear and they raced up the stairs and into their beds. Within moments there was a rap on the door. The three amigos pretended they were fast asleep. Then came a louder rap they could not possibly ignore and the question, "What were ye lads up to?"

"We're in bed."

"Open the door."

Charlie McCarthy nonchalantly walked to the door, pretending to rub the sleep from his eyes as he let the two mentors in, "What's the problem, Jim? We were fast asleep."

Jim looked at him with steely eyes, "Is that so? Jaysus, Charlie you're the only man I know to wear a collar and tie in bed."

Missed Opportunities

Waterford Manager, Justin McCarthy, was less than impressed by a fringe player with the team. He said to him, "It's a pity you didn't take up the game sooner."

"You mean I'd be better now?"

"No, you would have given up the game long ago."

Parting Shot

In terms of hurlers Justin McCarthy said, "You know when a player is great coming to the end of his career. A great player when he is gone will never be forgotten. A bad player is one who is not yet gone but is already forgotten!"

Blooming Disgrace

When Anthony Daly opened his new sports shop in Ennis he received a bouquet of flowers. He became dismayed on reading the enclosed card, that it expressed 'Deepest Sympathy'.

While puzzling over the message; his telephone rang. It was the florist, apologizing for having sent the wrong card.

"Oh, it's alright," said the greatest captain in modern times. "I'm a businessman and I understand how these things can happen."

"But," added the florist, "I accidentally sent your card to a funeral party."

"Well, what did it say?" asked Daly.

"Congratulations on your new location," was the reply!

Hurlers Off The Pitch

Hurling managers down through the years have been known to produce and inspire some magnificent moments as the following selection illustrates:

"Ger Loughnane isn't here today, which strongly suggests he might be somewhere else."

CYRIL FARRELL

"There are guys up there on the Council who want change? They couldn't even spell the word."

EAMON CREGAN ON THE CENTRAL COUNCIL

"We need to look at more bottoms-up in hurling."

LIAM GRIFFIN

"Never watch a Gaelic football match before hurling as it slows the mental reflexes."

MENTOR TO CORK TEAM IN THE 1960S

"I have never seen an organisation so hidebound by bullshit."

LIAM GRIFFIN ON THE GAA

"And as for you. You're not even good enough to play for this shower of useless no-hopers."

FORMER CLARE MENTOR TO ONE OF HIS SUBS AFTER A HEAVY DEFEAT

"Well, it's Clare 1-14 and Wexford 0-8, and if the score stays this way, I've got to fancy Clare for the win."

LIAM GRIFFIN

"He had an eternity to play that ball, but took too long."

LIAM GRIFFIN

"Knowing what goes on in Justin McCarthy's head is a bigger mystery than the third secret of Fatima."

WATERFORD FAN

"When Donal O'Grady smiles you can hear the cello in Jaws."

KEITH DUGGAN IN *THE IRISH TIMES* (SEPT 13, 2003)

"Loughnane had us coming out of that dressing-room with smoke coming out of our backsides."

ANTHONY DALY ON THE BUILD-UP TO THE MATCH AGAINST CORK IN 1998

"Hurlers do not stop playing because they were old: they grow old because they stop playing."

LIAM GRIFFIN

"They look like world beaters going forward and panel-beaters in the defence."

CYRIL FARRELL ON GALWAY IN 2005

"It was a pressure shot for Jamesie with Sean Óg breathing down his throat."

CYRIL FARRELL

"That could have made it a five points lead and there's a subtle difference between that and four points."

CYRIL FARRELL

"An ounce of breeding is worth a tonne of feeding."

OUSTED CLARE BOSS, TONY CONSIDINE, REFLECTS ON THE INTRODUCTION OF BARRY LOUGHNANE, GER'S SON, AGAINST LAOIS IN THE 2007 QUALIFIERS

SIX

GAA Management Made Simple

Gaelic games, especially when they involve managing a county team, are a very interesting and curious sociological phenomenon, with their own specialized vocabulary. Many fans do not fully appreciate the nuances of these words. The following glossary of terms may help readers understand them better.

METICULOUS ATTENTION TO DETAIL:
A nit picker

HAS LEADERSHIP QUALITIES:
Is tall or has a loud voice

EXCEPTIONALLY GOOD JUDGMENT:
Lucky

STRONG PRINCIPLES:
Stubborn

CAREER-MINDED:
Back-stabber

RELAXED ATTITUDE:
Sleeps on the job

PLANS FOR ADVANCEMENT:
Buys drinks for all the lads at happy hour

TAKES PRIDE IN WORK:
Conceited

FORCEFUL:
Argumentative

AGGRESSIVE:
Obnoxious

USES LOGIC ON DIFFICULT JOBS:
Gets someone else to do it

A KEEN ANALYST:
Thoroughly confused and confusing

OF GREAT VALUE TO THE ASSOCIATION:
Gets to training on time

EXPERIENCED PROBLEM SOLVER:
Screws up often

THE GAA IS HIS FIRST PRIORITY:
He's too ugly to get a date

FORWARD THINKING:
Procrastinator

INDEPENDENT WORKER:
Nobody knows what he does all day

GREAT PRESENTATION SKILLS:
Able to bullsh*t well

GOOD COMMUNICATION SKILLS 1:
Spends a lot of time on phone

GOOD COMMUNICATION SKILLS 2:
Management communicates: you listen, figure out what they want and do it

MUST BE DEADLINE-ORIENTATED:
We're already way behind schedule

DUTIES WILL VARY:
Anyone can boss you around

A COMPLEX PERSONALITY:
A complete nut

SOME OVERTIME REQUIRED:
Some time each night and every weekend

SEEKING CANDIDATES WITH A WIDE VARIETY OF EXPERIENCE:
*You'll need it to replace the three guys who've just
left in a huff*

PROBLEM-SOLVING SKILLS A MUST:
You're walking into a team in perpetual chaos

REQUIRES TEAM LEADERSHIP SKILLS:
*You will have the responsibilities of management, without
the pay or respect*

LOYAL:
Can't get a job anywhere else

AVERAGE ABILITIES:
Not too bright

EXCEPTIONALLY WELL QUALIFIED:
Made no major blunders – YET

ACTIVE SOCIALLY:
Drinks a lot

FAMILY IS ACTIVE SOCIALLY:
Spouse drinks, too

CHARACTER ABOVE REPROACH:
Still one step ahead of the Gardaí

ZEALOUS ATTITUDE:
Opinionated

QUICK THINKING:
Offers plausible excuses for mistakes

CAREFUL THINKER:
Won't make a decision

KEEN SENSE OF HUMOUR:
Knows a lot of dirty jokes

EXPRESSES THEMSELVES WELL:
Speaks English good

CONSCIENTIOUS:
Scared

FAIR:
Says that referees are only human, he thinks

INDEPENDENT:
Needs no assistance because is perfectly capable of messing up on his own

CASUAL WORK ATMOSPHERE:
We don't pay you enough to expect that you will dress up

APPLY IN PERSON
If you're too old or too ugly or too whatever, you will be told the position has been filled

Cracking The Code

Of course managers resort to a particularly sophisticated code to describe players. Below is just a representative sample:

HE IS A UNIQUE TALENT:
Sure he couldn't kick snow off a rope

HE ALWAYS MAKES THE BALL DO THE WORK:
He is lazy

HE COULD GET MORE OUT OF THE BALL.
He is stupid

HE HAS TO TRAIN A LITTLE BIT HARDER:
He is completely unfit

IN FAIRNESS HE HAS A POWERFUL SHOT:
He never hits the target

HE WAS A GREAT MINOR:
He has not played a good game since he was sixteen

HE IS A GOOD GRAFTER:
He is a carthorse, a player with no skill, to be brought on as a sub at corner forward, usually when the team is four goals down and playing against the wind and has not a chance of winning

SEVEN

My Kingdom Come

Although July 2007 saw Páidí O'Shea's career in management taking a temporary halt when he stepped down as Clare 'Supremo' his passion for football was evident at an early stage, dating back to when Kerry beat Meath in the 1970 All-Ireland Final. Páidí was a boarder so it was not possible for him to legitimately attend the homecoming celebrations. He arranged to borrow a bike from one of the day students, robbed a brush and dressed it up as a decoy in his bed and set out for Rathmore. When he returned the College Dean, Dermot Clifford, now Archbishop of Cashel was waiting for him at the entrance. "O Sé, there are more brains in that brush above than in your head."

Do Not Disturb

Páidí is a good story-teller and is well able to tell stories against himself. Many go back to his time as a Garda. In 1979 after a league match against Cork, he went on the tear. The next morning when he went into report for duty in Limerick he was feeling a bit off colour. He decided that the best way of concealing his discomfort was to take out the squad car and pretend to go on patrol but instead he pulled into a quiet field for a nap. A few hours later he was awoken by a great commotion and suddenly there were squad cars all over the field. Páidí stumbled out of the car to find himself face to face with the Assistant Commissioner who said, "Páid, did you nod off for a little while?"

"I'm sorry. I'd an auld game yesterday and I just pulled in for a few minutes. What are all of ye doing here?"

"We're checking out the venue for the Pope's visit to Limerick next September. The Holy Father'll be saying a Mass out here. We're sussin out the place for the security plan. Sorry to have disturbed you."

Nose-y

When Dublin played Kerry in 1978 as a fund-raiser for Sr Consilio, the match was the most physically violent in living memory. A lot of old scores had to be settled and markers were put down for the Championship later that year. A Dublin player broke Jimmy Deenihan's nose. Afterwards the Dub was very contrite and sent an apology later that night to Deenihan in the Kerry hotel. He told him he was very sorry and never intended to hurt him because he thought he was striking Páidí O'Sé!

Player Power

In 1985 everyone on the Kerry team had their heart set on winning the All-Ireland again. None more so than Páidí, as he was captain. As Páidí was trying to gee up the troops before the game he said: "We really need to win this one."

Mick O'Dwyer asked: "For who?"

"For me."

"Not for Kerry?"

"Well, for Kerry as well."

In an effort to add impact to his words Páidí smashed the ball as hard as he could on the ground. It bounced so high that it shattered the lights overhead. Glass flew all over the dressing-room. Yet so absorbed were the team in the team talk that not a single player noticed the incident.

Legacy

As a close friend of the late Charlie Haughey it is not surprising that Páidí loves verbal jousting. He has already left a rich legacy to GAA folklore as the source and object of some quotes that will live long in the memory. These include:

> Clare fan: "Is the glass half-empty or half-full?"
> Páidí: "It depends on whether you're drinking or pouring."

> "We're just off for a quiet pint. Then about twenty loud ones."

> "They think we're just a crowd of ignorant culchies from the bog. Let's not disappoint them."

PÁIDÍ PSYCHES UP KERRY BEFORE FACING THE DUBS

DAVID HICKEY (BEFORE DUBLIN PLAYED KERRY IN 1975):
"Welcome to Hell."
Páidí O'Shea: "True but meet the Devil."

DESSIE DOLAN BEFORE A FLIGHT:
"Look here Páidí if it's your day to go, it's your day to go."
Páidí: "But if it's the fuck**g pilot's day to go, he's going to bring me down with him!"

Páidí to Westmeath player: "For f**k's sake, will you go up for the ball."
Player: "Sure won't it come down to me."

Last Orders

Páidí always enjoyed the social side of the game. In the 1970s and 1980s winning All-Irelands became such a routine that as they ran on to Croke Park after Mick O'Dwyer had been trying to psyche the Kerry players up to play the game of their lives before an All-Ireland final, John Egan ran up and pulled Páidí O Sé by the togs and asked him, "Where are ye going after the game, Páid?"

In The Hot Seat

Páidí's finest hour as a manager came when he led Kerry to the 1997 All-Ireland. That was the game when Maurice Fitzgerald regularly broke through the Mayo defenders falling around him like dying wasps and kicked incredible points from all angles. There was a time Pat Spillane would have joked that if his mother had been marking Pat Holmes that day she would have been man of the match.

Not any more! After a replay against Galway he led them to another All-Ireland in 2000.

The wheels came off the wagon though in the 2001 All-Ireland semi-final when Meath beat Kerry by no less than 15 points. Kerry went through a 29 minute spell in the first half without scoring and then could only muster a single point from substitute Declan Quill in the second half. After the match Marty Morrissey asked a Kerry fan: "Where did it all go wrong in Croke Park today?"

The fan replied: "The green bit in the middle."

Worse was to come the next year when Kerry appeared to be cruising to the All-Ireland Final at half-time but to Kerry fans their team let Armagh snatch victory from the jaws of defeat. Immediately the joke was told: "Why aren't the Kerry team allowed to own a dog?"

"Because they can't hold on to a lead."

When it seemed that things could get no worse Kerry people sat at home the following year and watched Tyrone destroy the Kingdom in the All-Ireland semi-final. Two Tralee men had a revealing conversation: "I saw the Kerry team on television last night with the Sam Maguire trophy."

"What programme was it?"

"*Crimeline*."

More Than Words

2003 was Páidí's year of the U-turn. In January he gave an interview with *The Sunday Independent* in January and famously said: "Being the Kerry Manager is probably the hardest job in the world because Kerry people, I'd say, are the roughest type of f*****g animals you could deal with. And you can print that."

A short time later he was forced to meekly apologise: "I regret very much if I have offended all or some of my Kerry supporters who have been very loyal to me."

Marooned

When he became manager of Westmeath in 2004, apart from his strong language, some of the players found Páidí's stories a little baffling. One was about the seaman who met a pirate and noticed that he had a peg leg, a hook and an eye patch. "So how did you end up with a peg leg?" the seaman asked. "I was swept overboard and a shark bit my leg off," the pirate replied. "What about your hook?" asked the seaman. "Well, we were boarding an enemy ship and one of the enemy cut my hand off," the pirate said.

"So how did you get the eye patch?" the seaman finally asked.

"I got something in my eye," replied the pirate. When the sailor looked confused, the pirate continued: "It was my first day with the hook."

To this day the Westmeath players are still trying to figure out what point he was trying to make with the story.

Sour Grapes

Páidí has his critics and sometimes they don't pull their punches:

"Páidí O'Sé took the defeat very badly – so badly in fact that on the Tuesday of the defeat he rang the Samaritans. When they heard who it was they hung up."

CLARE FAN AFTER LOSING TO WATERFORD IN 2007

"In Kerry we have not had much to be proud of but we like to think Páidí is the greatest magician of all time. He made Kerry disappear for the entire second half of the 2002 All-Ireland Final against Armagh."

KERRY FAN

"He's not so much a coach as a hearse."

A FRUSTRATED MAURICE FITZGERALD FAN ON PÁIDÍ O SÉ

"Kerry's nickname should no longer be 'The Kingdom' but 'The Animal Kingdom'."

CORK FAN AFTER THE 'F**KING ANIMALS' CONTROVERSY

"In future Cork should in future play all their home games against Kerry in Fota Wild Life Park to make the Kerry fans feel at home."

ANOTHER CORK FAN ON THE SAME ISSUE

EIGHT

Players, Power and Poetry

Without great players there could be no Gaelic games. We are lucky to have so many great entertainers on every level. As a young man apart from football Meath star and a General Election candidate in 2007 Graham Geraghty, was more interested in romance than politics. At one point he was very much in love with a beautiful girl. One day she told him that the next day was her birthday. He told her he would send her a bouquet of roses – one for each year of her life. That evening he called the local florist and ordered 21 roses with instructions that they be delivered first thing the next morning.

As the florist was preparing the order, he decided that since the young man was such a good customer, he would put an extra dozen roses in the bouquet. It was years later before Geraghty found out what made the young woman so angry with him.

Love Hurts

In 1995 Jason Sherlock became the GAA's first pin-up boy as Dublin went on to the All-Ireland. With his sex appeal Jayo was a big hit with ladies. After his goal which beat Cork in the All-Ireland semi-final, the Cork fans were keen to have a pop at him. In their version of his romantic life Jayo fell for a girl and they got serious. Shortly after she told him that they couldn't afford to drink beer anymore and that he would have to quit. A few weeks later he caught her spending £50 on make-up. He asked her why he had to give up stuff but she didn't. She said she needed the make-up to look pretty for him. He told her that was what the beer was for. The relationship ended there and then.

Flying Without Wings

Great players have to be careful what they wish for. Peter Canavan and Eoin Mulligan died and went to Heaven. St Peter greeted them, and said, "I'm sorry, gentlemen, but your mansions aren't ready yet. Until they are, I can send you back to earth as whatever you want to be."

"Great," said Canavan, "I want to be an eagle soaring above beautiful scenery."

"No problem," replied St Peter, and POOF! Peter the Great was gone. "And what do you want to be," St Peter asked Mulligan.

"I'd like to be one cool stud!" was the reply.

"Easy," replied St Peter, and Mulligan was gone.

After a few months, their mansions were finished, and St Peter sent an angel to fetch them back. "You'll find them easily," he said, "One of them is soaring above the Grand Canyon, and the other one is on the bottom of a fridge in Omagh."

A Broad Canvas

One of the great contributions of footballers to Irish life is that they have been the stimulus for a wide range of reflections on a wide variety of topics such as:

"Football and sex are so utterly different. One involves sensuality, passion, emotion, commitment, selflessness, the speechless admiration of sheer heart-stopping beauty, rushes of breathtaking, ecstatic excitement, followed by shattering, toe-curling, orgasmic pleasure. And the other is sex."

JOE O'CONNOR

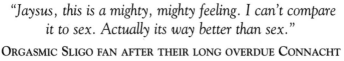

"Jaysus, this is a mighty, mighty feeling. I can't compare it to sex. Actually its way better than sex."

ORGASMIC SLIGO FAN AFTER THEIR LONG OVERDUE CONNACHT TITLE IN 2007

"The whole point about death, metaphorically speaking, is that it is almost bound to occur before the major trophies have been awarded."

KERRY FAN

"Last guys don't finish nice."

FRUSTRATED LEITRIM FAN

"Why did they not take off their pyjamas?"

**A YOUNG BOY TO HIS FATHER IN 1960 WATCHING DOWN
BECAME THE FIRST INTER-COUNTY TEAM TO WEAR TRACKSUITS**

"Leitrim for Croke Park: Mayo for Croagh Patrick."

**SIGN OUTSIDE A CHURCH IN LEITRIM AFTER THEIR HISTORIC
CONNACHT TITLE IN 1994**

"Frankie goes to Hollywood."

**MAYO FAN'S REACTION TO FRANKIE DOLAN'S 'THEATRICALS'
WHICH 'CAUSED' A MAYO PLAYER TO BE SENT OFF IN THE
CONNACHT FINAL IN 2001. HIS COMMENTS ON THE TWO
ROSCOMMON PLAYER'S TALENT FOR PLAYING POOL IN THE
NUDE CANNOT BE REPRINTED ON THE GROUNDS OF THE
DECENCY LAWS**

"In terms of the Richter scale, this defeat was a force 8 gale."

MEATH FAN AFTER THE 2001 ALL-IRELAND FINAL

"The grub in the hotel was the only good thing about the day."

NEMO RANGERS FAN AFTER THE 2002 ALL-IRELAND CLUB FINAL

"I'm going to tape The Angelus over this."

MEATH FAN ON RECEIVING THE VIDEO RECORDING OF THE 2001 ALL-IRELAND FINAL

"It gives a whole new meaning to powder your nose."

FANS REACTION TO A RUMOUR THAT A PLAYER WAS REACTING TO PRESSURE BY TAKING COCAINE

"The GAA is an amateur association run by professionals. The FAI is a professional body run by amateurs."

FAN DURING THE ROY KEANE WORLD CUP SAGA

"I never knew Solidarity had such popular support in Cork."

REMARK ATTRIBUTED TO GARRET FITZGERALD WHEN HE ARRIVED IN CORK ON A SUNDAY AND SAW HORDES OF PEOPLE SWATHED IN RED AND WHITE, AT A TIME WHEN THE SOLIDARITY MOVEMENT IN POLAND WAS AT ITS ZENITH, NOT REALIZING THEY WERE ON THEIR WAY TO A MUNSTER CHAMPIONSHIP MATCH

Mistaken Identity

In the early 90s a certain club in Cavan were facing an Intermediate relegation game. They fielded a ringer – a Meath county footballer, who a few years earlier had won an All-Ireland senior medal. He played under an assumed name. He caught the ball on his own forty, went on a solo run and scored a sensational point. One of the opposition management said: "Jaysus, that lad is brilliant. He should be on the county team." His opposing chairman muttered under his breath: "He is."

After Cavan lost to Tyrone a few years ago in a match they should have won in the Ulster Championship the Cavan fans were dejected. Cavan's Cathal Collins had not had a good game and as he trooped wearily off the field the

Cavan fans started shouting at him: "They shot the wrong Collins."

Ross Goes Shopping

After Longford lost to Laois in the 2007 Championship Laois star Ross Mulleny went to Granard and as he parked his car a Longford fan came over to him and suggested that he give him money to mind his car while he went into the shop. Ross reassured him that this was not necessary because he had a dog in his car. Quick as a flash the fan replied: "Yeah, but can he put out a fire?"

Another day Ross was going into a supermarket in Portarlington and was a bit unnerved when this elderly woman kept staring at him. Eventually she came over to him and said she reminded him of her son, who had died tragically the previous Christmas. She got very upset and then pulled out a picture of her son. Ross did not think he looked a bit like him – especially as he was Chinese! Nonetheless he went along with her and agreed he was the cut of him. This seemed to cheer her up. Then she said there was one thing that he could do that would mean a lot to her if he let her say: "Goodbye son," as she left the shop. Although Ross was a bit uncomfortable with the idea he said, "Okay." He got on with his few purchases and as he was picking up his newspapers he heard the woman shouting over at him: "Goodbye son," and waving at him furiously. He gave her a wave back. A few minutes later he was paying for his purchases and was shocked when the assistant told him that his total was over 500 euro. Ross was expecting it to be just under 20 euro and was flabbergasted. He asked her how the bill could be so high. She told him: "Oh your mother said you would pay for her groceries also!"

Go To Hell

After Donegal dramatically beat Armagh with a late goal in the 2007 Ulster Championship the frustrated Armagh fans told a joke about the Donegal legend Adrian Sweeney. The big Donegal forward dies and meets Satan in a room with three doors. Satan explains, "I have good news and bad news. The bad news is that you have to spend eternity behind one of these doors. But, the good news is that you have a peek behind each and take your choice."

So, Sweeney opened the first door and saw a room full of people, standing on their heads on a concrete floor. Not very nice, he thought. Opening the second door, he saw a room full of people standing on their heads on a wooden floor. Better he thought, but best to check the last door. Upon opening the last door, he saw a room full of people, standing waist-deep in excrement and sipping coffee.

"Of the three, this one looks best," he said and waded in to get something to drink while Satan closed the door. A few minutes later the door opened, Satan stuck his head in and said, "Ok, coffee break's over, back on your heads."

Glamour

The fact that forwards have featured so prominently in this chapter indicates that they are in the glamour position in Gaelic football. Accordingly, they have been the source and subject of a number of humorous quotations including:

> *"Somebody should check his birth cert because I don't think he was born, I think he's a creation of God."*

COLM O'ROURKE ON THE APPARENTLY DIVINE
COLM 'GOOCH' COOPER

"I used to think it was great being a wee nippy corner forward, but it's better now being a big, burly one."

MEATH ACE OLLIE MURPHY

"He simply wished us well for the second half and hoped the awful weather would improve."

DENIS ALLEN'S EDITED VERSION OF WHAT MICKY KEARINS SAID TO HIM AND DUBLIN CAPTAIN, GERRY HARGAN, WHEN HE PULLED THE CAPTAINS ASIDE BEFORE THE START OF THE SECOND HALF AND INSTRUCTED THEM TO WARN THEIR PLAYERS ABOUT THEIR BEHAVIOUR IN THE 1989 ALL-IRELAND SEMI-FINAL AFTER A VERY PHYSICAL FIRST HALF

Paddy McCormack digging a hole along the ground with his boot: "You're young Kearins, from Sligo. I presume you expect to go back to Sligo this evening."
Micheál Kearins: "Hopefully."
McCormack: "If you don't pass the mark, you have a fair chance of getting back."

"Some players are consistent. Some players are brilliant, but Micheál Kearins was consistently brilliant."

MICHEÁL O'MUIRCHEARTAIGH

"Mayo always had a big problem coping with being favourites and never lost it!"

FORMER MAYO STAR, WILLIE MCGEE

"They said we were like the British Army, that we lose our power when we cross the border, but we've proved we have power today."

PETER CANAVAN AS HE LIFTED THE SAM MAGUIRE CUP

"I was the non-playing captain!"

DINNY ALLEN AFTER HE CAPTAINED THE CORK TEAM TO WIN THE ALL-IRELAND IN 1989. A LOT OF HURLERS ON THE DITCH ALLEGED THAT ALLEN HADN'T CONTRIBUTED MUCH TO WINNING SAM!

Kilmore player trying to trick Tony Mc: "Tony, Tony, pass the ball to me."
Tony McManus: "Even if I was playing with you, I wouldn't pass you the ball!"
"The first time I got the ball I passed it to a teammate and raced on to take the return pass but instead he booted the ball two miles in the air!"

IGGY JONES ON HIS TYRONE DEBUT

"They are in the graveyard."

JIMMY KEAVENEY WHEN ASKED WHAT HAPPENED TO ALL THE GREAT KERRY FOOTBALLERS DURING THEIR 'FAMINE DAYS' IN THE EARLY 90S

"Those guys are going to be bleeding all over us."

CORK PLAYER RESPONDS TO THE SIGHT OF A VERY HEAVILY BANDAGED WILLIE JOE PADDEN IN THE 1989 ALL-IRELAND FINAL

*"Don't be so modest [Padraic] Joyce. You're not t
hat great."*

WESTMEATH FAN DURING WESTMEATH'S SHOCK DEFEAT OF
GALWAY IN 2006

*"Jaysus, if Lee Harvey Oswald was from Mayo: JFK
would still be alive."*

MAYO FAN TO CONOR MORTIMER DURING THE
2006 ALL-IRELAND FINAL

"Well you can't blame me. I never got near the ball!"

A CORNER-FORWARD DISCLAIMS RESPONSIBILITY FOR A HEAVY
DEFEAT IN A CLUB GAME IN MAYO

*"Even Iarnród Éireann don't carry as many passengers as
we saw today."*

COLM O'ROURKE'S VERDICT ON THE DUBLIN AND OFFALY
FORWARDS IN THE 2007 LEINSTER SEMI-FINAL

"If Dublin win, it's over-hyped; if Dublin lose, it's over-hyped."

CIARAN WHELAN

Dynasty

It is not unusual in Gaelic games, as in politics, for famous footballers to produce equally famous sons. One of the most recent recruits to this motley crew is Mayo centre half-back Billie Joe Padden, whose father Willie Joe was one of the stars of the 1980s. As a young man though Billie Joe was always inclined to put his love of football first, to the detriment of his household chores. One day neighbours were shocked to see Willie Joe faint as he came out of his front door onto the porch. Someone rang 999. When the ambulance men arrived, they helped him regain consciousness and asked if he knew what caused him to faint.

"It was enough to make anybody faint," he said. "My son asked me for the keys to the garage, and instead of driving the car out, he came out with the lawn mower."

Salmon Leap

In the early 1990s Connacht footballers were invariably free in August and September and many took the route of weekend tourist for trans-Atlantic games.

Before their glory days of 1998 Galway were knocked out early in the Championship one year and a famous man in the GAA in New York, Jackie Salmon, rang Val Daly and asked him to travel over to line out for

Connemara Gaels the following Sunday and to bring a couple of other good players with him. Daly rang around and persuaded former Galway full-forward Brian O'Donnell to travel with him. Brian had never played in a match in New York. The two lads flew out on the Friday evening and on the plane Daly briefed his colleague on how to get through the weekend. He said, "Now Brian they do things differently over there. It's not like at home, so just enjoy the weekend, play the match and don't mind what anyone says. Whatever you do – say nothing."

The Tribesmen enjoyed the first part of the weekend but the match went less well. At half-time the Connemara Gaels were seven points down. Jackie Salmon gave a team-talk and said, "Ye're the most disgraceful shower I ever saw. Ye're a disgrace to the Connemara Gaels jersey. As for the big shots from over in Ireland I'm sorry I brought ye out at all. Daly you were hopeless and O'Donnell you were even worse. You didn't even catch one ball."

O'Donnell forgot Daly's advice and retorted, "Sure how could ye play football out there. There wasn't a single blade of grass on the pitch."

Salmon turned around to him and asked, "Did you come out here to play football or to graze?"

The Bitter Word

No matter how famous the name, fans too are no respecter of reputation as is clear from the following quotes:

Jack Mahon: "I played at centre half-back on the Galway team in 1956."
Fan: "Gosh that's shocking."
Jack: "Why?"
Fan: "Because I've just discovered my Dad's a liar. He's always said that when Galway won that All-Ireland they never had a centre-back!"

"My Dad told me you were the man that lost the All-Ireland for Tyrone!"

YOUNG FAN TO IGGY JONES

"He'll regret this to his dying day, if he lives that long."

DUBS FAN AFTER CHARLIE REDMOND MISSED A PENALTY IN THE 1994 ALL-IRELAND FINAL

"He [Colin Corkery] is as useless as a back pocket in a vest."

KERRY FAN

"Colin Corkery is deceptive. He's slower than he looks."

KERRY FAN

Q: "What's the difference between Paddy Cullen and a turnstile?"

A: "A turnstile only lets in one at a time."

KERRY FAN AFTER CULLEN CONCEDED FIVE GOALS IN THE 1978 ALL-IRELAND FINAL

Q. "What's the difference between Paddy Cullen and Cinderella?"

A: "At least Cinderella got to the ball."

KERRY FAN AFTER CULLEN WAS LOBBED BY MIKEY SHEEHY IN THE SAME MATCH

"Leitrim football fan shouting abuse at one of their corner backs: "Take that useless c**t off, he's good for nothing." Another fan: "That's terribly insulting. Imagine if he was your son."
"That useless f***er is my son!"

"We call him Cinderella because he kept missing the ball."

LEITRIM FAN ON A FORMER GOALKEEPER

"Actually he should be called Dracula because he is terrified of crosses."

ANOTHER LEITRIM FAN ON THE SAME GOALIE

New Rules

Glen Ryan is one of the true legends of Kildare football. He has a share in a pub in Newbridge. In the late 1990s when Kildare had a very keen rivalry with Meath it was rumoured that there was a sign in the pub which read, 'No Meath supporters served in this pub'. One day a man draped in the Meath colours came into the bar, "I know you don't serve Meath supporters, but I'm desperate for a drink and I'll pay £5 for a pint."

The barman thought this over, then decided to serve the pint. It was gulped down in one go. "Same again," said the Meath fan, "in fact I'll have two," and he slapped a tenner on the bar. After a few minutes he asked for another. The barman said tentatively, "That's another fiver?"

"That's okay," he said, pushing a £50 note across the bar, "I'll have a couple for the road. Keep the change."

When the drinker had gone the barman put up a new sign: 'Only Meath fans served here'.

Oh Brother Where Art Thou?

Paddy 'Bawn' Brosnan was one of the all time great Kerry footballers. His commitment to football was evident at an early age. Attending the local Christian Brothers school he was asked to conjugate the Latin verb '*venio*'. Paddy Bawn simply shrugged his shoulders and said, "Ah sure Brother, I'm only here for the football."

Mighty Meath

In the 70s Dublin's great rivals were Kerry but in the late 1980s and 1990s their most intense rivalry was with Meath. In 1983 after Dublin won the All-Ireland they travelled to Navan for the opening round of the National League. The All-Ireland champions were welcomed onto the field by the Meath team lined either side of the dug-out. While the team applauded the Dubs, a Meath player was caught by one photographer giving the champs the two fingers!

The popular perception of Meath football is probably best captured in the following quotes:

"You can't make an omelette without breaking legs."

A MEATH FAN MADE AN INTERESTING AND REVEALING SLIP OF THE TONGUE IN 1996 AFTER THE ALL-IRELAND SEMI-FINAL WHEN TYRONE FANS WERE LOUD IN THEIR CONDEMNATION OF THE MEATH TEAM, PARTICULARLY OF THEIR ALLEGED ILL-TREATMENT OF PETER CANAVAN

"The rules of Meath football are basically simple - if it moves, kick it; if it doesn't move, kick it until it does."

TYRONE FAN AFTER CONTROVERSIAL ALL-IRELAND SEMI-FINAL IN 1996

"Meath make football a colourful game - you get all black and blue."

CORK FAN IN 1987

"Meath players like to get their retaliation in first."

CORK FAN IN 1988

Barred

When Dublin played Meath in the 1996 Leinster Final Meath's Tommy Dowd was in a clash of heads with Dublin's Keith Barr. Some time later Keith's brother, Johnny, was also in the wars with Tommy. After the match Tommy was going up for an interview when he banged his head against a bar in one of the barriers – an injury which subsequently necessitated four stitches. As he held his head in agony a passing Dublin fan said to him, "I see you made the hat-trick."

"What do you mean?" Tommy asked.

"Johnny Barr, Keith Barr and iron bar!"

No Objection

John B. Keane was a good footballer and a great admirer of
the pride people took in playing club football in Kerry and
told a story to illustrate. Within hours of the tragic death
of the corner-forward in a traffic accident, an ambitious
young hopeful rang the local Club Chairman. "I hope you
don't mind me ringing at this time," he said, "But I was
wondering whether I might take the place of the deceased
. . ."

"I hadn't really thought about it," replied the
Chairman, "but if the undertaker doesn't mind, then
neither will I."

Passion Play

John B. also recalled a famous Kerry footballer who went
on his honeymoon. As he watched his wife undress on
their wedding night the player uttered the most erotic line
in the history of Irish sport: "Your buttocks have me
intoxicated."

Fiercesome

John B. also told a story about a Kerry County Junior
Football final. By the time the final was played most of the
better players had returned to college as it was delayed due
to the usual quota of objections. John B. claimed he was
drafted in to play at corner forward, even though he was
only about 15 years of age. He gave a vivid description of
his increasing trepidation as he went to take up his
position and saw a 'seasoned' corner-back advancing to
meet him. John B. was getting more intimidated with each
step but was puzzled when the corner-back veered off at
the last moment and went back towards his goalkeeper.
He took out his false teeth and loudly told his keeper:

"Paddy, mind these in case I forget myself and eat someone."

Quote, Unquote

While Kerry footballers have given great entertainment down the years with their performances on the field sometimes their comments off it can be every bit as entertaining as the following compilation indicates:

"He was a man mountain – he would catch aeroplanes if it helped Kerry."

JOHN B. KEANE ON MICK O'CONNELL

"What they say about Cork footballers being ignorant is rubbish. I spoke to a couple yesterday and they were quite intelligent."

BRENDAN KENNELLY

"A Kerry footballer with an inferiority complex is one who thinks he's just as good as everybody else."

JOHN B. KEANE

"He [Mick O'Connell] hit it so hard that the ball burst on its journey. The cover of the ball landed outside the presbytery in Lisdoonvarna. The bladder landed outside a hoor house in Buenos Aires."

JOHN B. KEANE

"I had to go home to milk the cows."

MICK O'CONNELL, THE MAN FROM VALENTIA, WHEN ASKED WHY HE LEFT THE DRESSING-ROOM IMMEDIATELY AFTER CAPTAINING KERRY TO WIN THE ALL-IRELAND AND HEADED STRAIGHT HOME FOR KERRY

"How would you know a Cork footballer? He's the one who thinks that oral sex is just talking about it."

JOHN B. KEANE

"Referees are like wives, you can never tell how they're going to turn out."

JOHN B. KEANE

"Now listen lads, I'm not happy with our tackling. We're hurting them but they keep getting up."

JOHN B. KEANE VENTURES INTO COACHING

"If they won't take you off, for f**k's sake, walk off!"

KERRY FAN TO HIS OWN PLAYER DURING THE 2001 ALL-IRELAND SEMI-FINAL HUMILIATION TO MEATH

"A farmer could make a tidy living on the space of ground it takes Moss Keane to turn."

DANNY LYNCH ON MOSS KEANE'S LESS THAN RESOUNDINGLY SUCCESSFUL CAREER AS A GAELIC FOOTBALLER

"Keep your high balls low into the wind."

ADVICE TO A YOUNG JOHN B. KEANE

"Micky Joe made his championship debut in such a way that he will never be asked to make it again."

JOHN B. KEANE

Q: *"Why was Jesus born in Bethlehem and not in the Kerry dressing-room?"*
A: *"They would never have got three wise men in the Kerry dressing-room."*

"Karl O'Dwyer will go down in history as the rat who joined the sinking ship."

KERRY FAN ON KARL'S DEFECTION TO KILDARE

Q. *"What do Kerry footballers use for contraception?"*
A. *"Their personalities."*

The Iron Man

Paddy McCormack, 'The Iron Man from Rhode', was a tough man though the story goes that when he made his debut for Offaly his mother was concerned about the physical nature of the exchanges. She turned to her husband and said, "Poor Paddy will break a leg."

According to folklore her husband looked at her reproachfully and said, "He might but it won't be his own."

Extra Leg

Another story told about Paddy goes back to the time he had a terrible leg on him, returning to the dressing-room, after a bruising encounter in a National League match. It was covered in cuts and bruises and had a massive gash from the top of the thigh to the knee. He had no idea whose it was.

Jack The Lad

Armagh finally reached the Promised Land in 2002. One of their great personalities was their goalie, Benny Tierney. In 2003 Benny went to San Diego with the All-Stars. As part of the trip some of the tourists went to see a NBA basketball match. Among the attendance was legendary actor Jack Nicholson. At one point in the game there was a controversial call and Jack was incensed. He rose to his feet and started screaming at the officials. When the torrent of abuse died down Benny rose to his feet and reprised one of Nicholson's most famous roles, in *A Few Good Men*, when he shouted, "You want the truth? You can't handle the truth!"

Armagh's pre-match breakfast menu provided Benny with another classic quote: "It used to be a good old Ulster fry before matches, but we've changed that now to muesli – which tastes a wee bit like what you'd find at the bottom of a budgie's cage."

Nudie

One test of fame is when you are known simply by your first name: Bono, Gay, Sean Óg – no further introduction required. In Gaelic football circles the name 'Nudie' elicits instant recognition as that of Monaghan's most famous footballer; Eugene 'Nudie' Hughes. Nudie helped Monaghan to three Ulster Senior Football championships in 1979, 1985 and 1988.

Nudie was well able to hold his own in any company. One player who gave him a lot of problems though was the Kerry forward; John Egan. Ulster were playing a Railway Cup match against Munster and Nudie was marking John. They were standing talking because Nudie always talked to opponents even though he would be told not to. At one stage John said, "What's that man writing down on that piece of paper? He's a right looking eejit isn't he?" As Nudie turned to answer John was sticking the ball into the net.

In 1988 Nudie used that same trick on Cavan's Damien O'Reilly. He was marking him in the Ulster Final. At one stage in the game Nudie said, "Jaysus there's an awful lot of people up on the hill. How many people would you say is up there?" As Damien looked up to make his guess the ball came in between them and Nudie caught it without any obstruction and stuck it over the bar. O'Reilly was taken off him immediately.

Too Many Murphys

Nudie also made his mark on foreign shores. He played in England but his club game with Round Towers in New

Eltham was cancelled. A few enterprising men came up from Bristol and got Nudie to play against Gloucester in a league final, totally illegally. He was the last brought on and about to hand his name, 'Brian Murphy' to the ref. The official from Bristol called him back and said, "I'd better change that, as the other two I sent in were Brian Murphys and the ref would surely spot it." They changed it to Aidan Dempsey and went on to win the match.

Revised Orders

Three times All-Ireland winner Mick Higgins captained Cavan to an All-Ireland final victory in 1952. The first match ended in a draw. It was the first time the GAA brought the two teams together for a meal after the game. When Mick and some of the Cavan boys got to the hotel they ordered drinks – just bottles of ale and a mineral. Mick went to pay for it but the barman said it was on the GAA. Mick double checked if he had heard correctly. Quick as a flash once this was confirmed one of his colleagues said, "Forget about the ales and get us brandies." For the replay though there was no free drink!

Bonus Point

Some stories take hold of popular mythology which have just the faintest touches of credibility and therefore enter the canon of GAA legend. A case in point was the story of a match in 1957 when a new pitch was being opened in St Brendan's Hospital. As reigning All-Ireland Football Champions, Galway, were invited to play the home team and duly were awarded a penalty in the game. A Galway player, Mick Ford, who once scored a goal in a club hurling match in Dublin directly from a puckout, is said to have hit the ball so hard that the lace of the ball came undone and the leather part went over the bar and the bladder went into the net. As a result Galway were said to have been awarded a goal and a point!

Slim Pickings

One of the most prolific Longford goal-scorers in the game is not known for his lithe frame. After a bit of slagging about his waistline, he decided to go on a diet. It was one he took very seriously as was seen the night after training, he went into a chipper and ordered a quarter-pounder, double chips, onion rings and a smoked cod. When he ordered his can of coca-cola his good nutritional sense prevailed and he asked the assistant: "Could you make it a low-fat option please as I'm on a diet."

Captain Fantastic

As this book was being written, the death of one of Gaelic football's great gentlemen and characters, Dermot O'Brien, took place. He captained Louth to their only senior All-Ireland title in 1957. Of course he was equally famous for his powers on the accordion and his singing. As the two teams prepared to make their bold bids for glory before the 2007 All-Ireland I looked up to the heavens, convinced that the faint rumbling noise a corner of my brain had detected was the thundering of studs on the sky. I would like to think that Dermot O'Brien's and Jimmy Murray's teams were battling it out for the inaugural Heaven final. I would sacrifice my mortgage just to witness the outcome. The one difference though was that before this game, instead of playing the anthem, the Celestial boys' band played Dermot's biggest hit *The Merry Ploughboy*!

I Do, I Do, I Do

One of Dermot's favourite stories was about the Louth player of the 1950s who on a visit to America was chatted up by a woman in a bar. To put it very charitably; she was less than pretty and was as heavy as the combined weight of Louth's two midfielders. At first the Louth player was immune to the woman's charms. His attention though was captured when she told him that her mother had only two months to live and the dying widow had inherited a multi-million dollar fortune from her husband. Now the daughter stood to inherit everything. The Louth player was moved to action.

Two weeks later he was married . . . to the mother.

Tuff Stuff

Like their attacking counterparts, defences have also been the cause of many a funny quote including:

> *Fan: "So what's a forward doing playing in goal for Roscommon?"*
> *Shane Curran: "I'm trying to keep the ball out."*

> *"Is it any wonder we never won anything? The men on the County Board were so incompetent they couldn't even pick their own noses!"*
> FORMER WICKLOW STAR, GERRY O'REILLY

"They didn't drink like a fish. They drank like a shoal of mackerel."

AWESTRUCK FAN MARVELS AT THE DRINKING POWERS OF THE GREAT KERRY TEAM OF THE 1970S

"The midfield area was like New York City, going down Time Square, crazy."

SEAMUS MOYNIHAN AFTER KERRY LOST TO TYRONE IN 2003

"People slag me about my right leg but without it I couldn't use my left!"

JOHN MORLEY

"That's the first time I've seen anybody limping off with a sore finger!"

ARMAGH'S GENE MORGAN TO 'INJURED' TEAMMATE PAT CAMPBELL

"Kevin, keep close to the goal today. I didn't bring any oxygen!"

BILLY MORGAN EXPRESSING CONCERN ABOUT THE FITNESS OF HIS FULL-BACK, KEVIN KEHILLY

Journalist: "How's the leg Kevin?"
Kevin Moran: "It's very fuc . . . it's very sore."

AFTER THE 1978 ALL-IRELAND FINAL

Gravedigger pointing to the graves of all the famous Kerry footballers: "It's a very impressive collection, isn't it?"
Jack Bootham: "Tis indeed but the way things are going at the moment you'll have to dig them all up again if Kerry are ever going to win anything!"

"Do ye see this yoke, lads? I'm going to blow it now and blow it again at the finish and whatever happens in between ye can sort out yerselves."

NERVOUS REFEREE, POINTING TO HIS WHISTLE, TO THE TWO TEAMS BEFORE A CLUB GAME IN WICKLOW

"Francie Bellew marked so tight he would follow opponents to the dressing-room at half-time."

MARTIN McHUGH

"I don't want to sit on the fence, but this game could go either way."

PAUL CURRAN

Q: *"What's the difference between Francie Bellew and Kylie Minogue?"*
A: *"Francie marks tighter than Kylie's famous hotpants."*

"Graham Geraghty may not be sugar but he adds plenty of spice."

MEATH FAN

"The more stitches required after a game in the Cork dressing room, the more probable they had won."

CON MURPHY, CORK TEAM DOCTOR

NINE

Hurlers on and off the Pitch

"Ever since I started off in Na Piarsaigh, and going to the North Monastery, I was told Croke Park, the steps of the Hogan Stand – that's what you aspire to. I bought into that growing up on the northside of Cork, and I wanted to live that dream. And today it came true." When Sean Óg Ó hAilpín made his famous speech after captaining Cork to the All-Ireland hurling title in 2005 he immediately entered legendary status.

Nothing adorns the image of Gaelic games like a great hurler. The GAA can now boast its very own sex symbol in Sean Óg. When the Cork hurlers went on a team holiday to South Africa Sean Óg spent almost all of the vacation sunbathing on the roof of his hotel. He wore his trunks the first day, but on the second, he decided that no one could see him way up there, and he slipped out of it. He'd hardly begun when he heard someone running up the stairs. He was lying on his stomach, so he just pulled out a towel over his rear. "Excuse me, sir," said the flustered Assistant Manager of the Hotel, out of breath from running up the stairs. "The Hilton doesn't mind your sunbathing on the roof, but we would very much appreciate you wearing trunks as you did yesterday."

"What difference does it make?" Sean Óg asked rather

calmly. "No one can see me up here, and besides, I'm covered up with a towel."

"Not exactly," said the embarrassed Manager. "You're lying on the dining room skylight."

Sorry, Wrong Number

In the hurling hierarchy today there is perhaps nobody higher today than Tipperary's ace forward; Eoin Kelly. Limerick fans are less keen than others to sing his praises because of the keen rivalry between the two counties. They tell two stories about Kelly.

One morning the phone rang at 3.30 a.m. in Kelly's house. He picked up the phone and a woman asked, "Is this 4765489?"

"No, this is 4965488?" Kelly replied.

"Oh, I'm so sorry for disturbing you," the woman said.

"That's alright," Kelly said. "I had to get up to answer the phone anyway."

Another is about the time Kelly was trying to understand the nature of theology and asked: "God, how long is a million years to you?"

God was wearing his Limerick jersey and answered: "A million years is like a minute."

Then Kelly asked: "God, how much is million euros to you?"

And God replied: "A million euros is like a cent."

Finally, Kelly asked: "God, could you give me a cent?"

And God said, "In a minute."

Do The Maths

Kilkenny star JJ Delaney is one of the giants of hurling today but he is a very modest man. A gushy fan went up to him during a team golf outing: "You are spectacular;

your name is synonymous with the game of hurling and you're a great golfer too. You really know your way around the course. What's your secret?"

Delaney coolly replied: "The holes are numbered."

Limerick, You're A Lady

One of the stories of the hurling year has been the spectacular revival in the fortunes of Limerick hurling following years of internal discord. Under their own unique answer to Moses, Richie Bennis, Limerick regained their place at hurling's top table when they kept Dan the Man goalless and went on a five goal blitz of their own to qualify for the 2007 All-Ireland Hurling Final. After the game some cocky Shannonsiders were winding up the Waterford fans with a puzzle:

Q. *"How has Eddie Hobbs helped so many Waterford people to become millionaires?"*
A. *"He's got them to save all their money until after Waterford qualifies for an All-Ireland final."*

Til Death Do Us Part

Just when Dan Shanahan thought things could get no worse after losing the 2007 All-Ireland semi-final he sat through the final of *Charity You're A Star* and watched three GAA icons Jack O'Shea, David Beggy and Barney Rock bare almost all with their unique version of *The Full Monty*. Dan was in the company of a friend who was about to get married. The groom to be had just got a gift of cuff links from his beloved. As she works in a computer company one of the links was inscribed Ctrl (Control) and the other Esc (Escape). When he saw the cuff links Dan shook his head sadly and said: "It's the perfect gift for any new husband if only to remind him of two things he can never have again."

Fan-tasia

Believe it or not there a few people who can not appreciate hurling. Such disrespect offends the laws of nature and culture: "Hurling is cavemen's lacrosse," stated a British Sunday newspaper.

However, hurling fans down the years have been inspired by their heroes to produce a number of classic comments:

'Carlos Santana.'

THE NICKNAME GIVEN BY CARLTON AUSTRALIAN RULES CLUB FANS TO SETANTA Ó HAILPÍN. (THE CORK VERSION IS SIMPLY 'SANTY')

"The lion and the lamb shall lie down together, but the lamb won't get much sleep."

CLARE FAN ON ANY OPPONENT FACING UP TO BRIAN LOHAN

"I didn't get Christy Ring's autograph, but he trod on my toe, though."

CORK FAN

"Everyone knows which come first when it's a question of hurling or sex – all discerning people recognize that."

TIPP FAN

"Funny game hurling, especially the way Kerry play it."

COCKY CORK FAN

"We've won one All-Ireland in a row."

WEXFORD FAN IN 1996

"To be a great goalie, you need a big heart, big hands and a big bottom."

COMMENT ABOUT A FORMER ANTRIM GOALIE

"The man from Del Monte said 'Yes'."

DELIGHTED KILKENNY FAN AFTER DJ CAREY REVERSES HIS INITIAL DECISION TO RETIRE

"Pessimists see a cup that is half-empty: Optimists see a cup that is half-full. But we haven't even seen the cup."

SLIGO HURLING FAN

"Jesus saves – but Jimmy Barry-Murphy scores on the rebound."

GRAFFITI

"I love Cork so much that if I caught one of their hurlers in bed with my missus I'd tiptoe downstairs and make him a cup of tea."

JOE LYNCH

"He [Nicky English] spoilt the game – he got too many scores."

ANTRIM FAN AT THE 1989 ALL-IRELAND

"When Sylvie Linnane is good; he's great. When he's bad; he's better!"

GALWAY FAN

"It's all over . . . Clare are . . . Jeeesus."

MATTHEW McMAHON CLARE FM GAA COMMENTATOR REACTS TO CLARE'S MUNSTER FINAL TRIUMPH IN 1995

"The cigarettes are being lit here in the commentary box, the lads are getting anxious, it's a line ball down there to Clare and who's going to take it . . . Will ye put them out lads yee'll choke me."

MATTHEW MCMAHON DURING THE 95 ALL-IRELAND FINAL

"I'd say there's not one person in the stadium who went to the toilet today."

LARRY O'GORMAN

To Sir With Love

Jamesie O'Connor's mother always had some reservations about his decision to become a teacher. She rightly pointed out that at the time teachers were very respected but had very little money. She used to say that he would be better if he had a job with a little less respect and a little more money!

The Semplegate Eight

After the 'schemozzle' in Thurles between Cork and Clare in May 2007 and the decision to suspend eight players, the following conversation was overheard one morning in Mallow:

Father: "Son, what'll I buy you for your birthday?"
Son: "A bicycle."
Father: "What'll I buy you for your first communion?"
Son: "A playstation?"
Father: "What'll I buy you for Christmas?"
Son: "A Mickey Mouse outfit."
Father: "No problem son. I'll just buy you the GAA!"

Quirke-y

Carlow dual star's Paddy Quirke played senior football and hurling with the County in the 1970s and 1980s. The highlight of Quirke's career came when he was chosen as the dual All-Star replacement. He once played hurling in San Francisco and found it really tough and physical. At one stage he put in his hurley, angled with the bos to the ground, to block an opponent; got a severe belt across the face; was taken off and rushed to hospital. He had no social security cover, but his friends who were with him decided he was Patrick Foley (a genuine holder of social security). So all of a sudden he was somebody else. The only problem was when Paddy heard the name Patrick Foley being called out in the hospital he forgot that was supposed to be him and had to be reminded who he then was. At that stage he was not in very good shape and was expecting some sympathy from the doctor. Instead all he said was, "Were you playing that crazy Irish game?"

In 1985 Paddy played for his club Naomh Eoin against the Westmeath champions, Brownstown, in the first round of the Leinster Club Hurling Championship. One of his teammates was asked a few days later how bad the pitch was. He replied, "Well the grass was so long a hare rose at half time!"

Super Troupers

Hurling is the greatest game because of the thrills and spills on the pitch and the level of analysis off it. Cases in point include the following:

"Those guys in the media who wrote off Cork in the winter must have spent all their time watching Coronation Street."

CORK MIDFIELDER JERRY O'CONNOR RESPONDS TO CORK'S EASY WIN OVER CLARE IN 2007

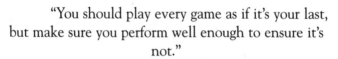

"You should play every game as if it's your last, but make sure you perform well enough to ensure it's not."

JACK LYNCH

"Sylvie Linnane: The man who drives a JCB on a Monday and turns into one on a Sunday."

GALWAY FAN

"It's hard to see the writing on the wall when your back is up against it."

SEAN ÓG Ó'HALPÍN ON THE 2006 ALL-IRELAND DEFEAT TO KILKENNY

"Football is a game for those not good enough to play hurling."

TONY WALL

"Cork are like the mushrooms; they can come overnight."

JIM 'TOUGH' BARRY

Nicky English shortly before the end of the 1988 All-Ireland: "How much time left ref?"
The ever helpful Sylvie Linnane: "At least another year for Tipperary!"

"Hurling – it's all a matter of inches; those between your ears."

ANTRIM'S KEVIN ARMSTRONG

"The only time in my playing days I heard anybody talking about hamstrings was when they were hanging outside a butcher's shop."

MICK 'RATTLER' BYRNE

"My innocent childhood perception of the priesthood changed after that game!"

SAMBO MCNAUGHTON RECALLS MARKING FR IGGY CLARKE ON HIS INTER-COUNTY DEBUT

"Hurling and sex are the only two things you can enjoy without being good at it."

JIMMY DEANE

"Why are Limerick magic? Because they can disappear for five minutes."

OFFALY FAN AFTER THE DRAMATIC 1994 ALL-IRELAND FINAL

"Broken marriages, conflicts of loyalty, the problems of everyday life fall away as one faces up to DJ Carey."

ANON WEXFORD PLAYER

Tales Of The Unexpected

Antrim's Dessie Donnelly has a special place in his heart for his teammates whose words are every bit as entertaining as their achievements. In 1989 after Antrim sensationally beat Offaly in the All-Ireland semi-final they were training hard coming up to the All-Ireland Final. To get a bit of a break Paul McKillen and Dessie went to see the All-Ireland football semi-final between Cork and Dublin. They were having a great chat before the game and as the players were coming on to the field Paul noticed the big screen for the first time and Dessie said to him, "This should be a great game today." Paul looked up at the big screen and then he turned around and asked Dessie, "Is this game live?" Donnelly nearly died laughing.

McKillen though is not the Antrim hurler who bought a JCB and set up his own business with the slogan, 'With us you're guaranteed your hole'.

The Oldest Swinger In Town

DJ Carey is well-known for his charity work and kindness. Sometimes though, people make unreasonable demands on him. One night he was awakened at 4 O'Clock in the morning by a loud pounding on the door. DJ got up and went down to the door where a drunken stranger stood in the pouring down rain. "Can you give me a push?" he asked while hanging onto the door frame.

"Not a chance," said DJ. "It's the middle of the night and its lashing drain." He slammed the door and was about to return to bed. But then he recalled getting help from a stranger when returning home from presenting medals to the Tremane Club in Roscommon so he went out into the pounding rain and called out into the dark, "Hello, are you still there?"

"Yes," came the answer.

"Do you still want a push?" called out DJ.

"Yes, please!" came the reply from the dark.

"Where are you?" asked DJ.

"Over here on the swing," the drunk replied.

Lord Of The Rings

Christy Ring is the prince of hurlers but he was a hard taskmaster. In the 1950s a Cork hurler was greeted, at the end of a disappointing performance in a Munster Championship match, with the frank appraisal of one Cork fan, "That was the worst display I ever saw by a Cork player. You were complete rubbish. In fact you were even worse."

The hurler, quite disturbed, informed Christy Ring what the man had said. Ring replied, "That poor chap is not really responsible for what he says. He never has an original thought. He just goes around repeating what everybody else is saying!"

Ring once met a young journalist on his way into an All-Ireland final. The journalist was trying to get information from him but Christy was more enigmatic than the Dead Sea Scrolls! Eventually the journalist lost patience and decided to quit while he still retained a shred of dignity and asked Christy one final question. "Can you tell me where to go for the press box?"

"To hell and back," Christy replied.

Christy once attended a match at Croke Park as a spectator. It was explained to him at the turnstiles that there were seats for £5, £10 and £20 and that programmes were half-a-crown.

"Okay," said Christy, "I'll sit on a programme."

Hurlers On The Ditch

Like their footballing counterparts hurlers have made some memorable comments such as the following:

Pat Carroll: "My hurley was stolen this morning."
Friend: "That's terrible – where did you lose it?"
Pat: "In the car-park."
Friend: "Did the thieves damage your car much."
Pat: "I don't know – they stole that too!"

I said to the manager, this is supposed to be a five-star hotel and there's a bloody hole in the roof. He turned around and said, "That's where you can see the five stars from."

PADDY QUIRKE ON ALL-STARS TOUR

"A fan is a person who, when you have made an idiot of
yourself on the pitch, doesn't think you've done a
permanent job."

JACK LYNCH

"A referee should be a man. They are for the most part
old women."

NICKY RACKARD

Mick 'Rattler' Byrne: "Don't be worrying Tommy. There
are two parachutes under the seat – you put one on; jump
out; count to ten; press the button, and you jump to
safety. What could be simpler?"
A nervous Tommy Doyle on a flight to New York: "But
what happens if the parachute doesn't open?"
"That's easy. You just jump back up and get the
spare one."

"To tell you the truth I'd rather if he had won a Munster medal!"

FORMER TIPPERARY STAR, BILLY QUINN IN 1990 TO A JOURNALIST WHEN HE WAS ASKED IF HE WAS PROUD OF HIS SON, NIALL, WHO SCORED THE GOAL AGAINST HOLLAND IN ITALIA 90

"I was only doing Babs Keating!"

A TEN YEAR-OLD NIALL QUINN AFTER SHATTERING HIS KITCHEN WINDOW TO SMITHEREENS WITH HIS SLÍOTAR WHEN PRACTICING HIS FREES

Rattler Byrne: "By God, Christy, we'll have to shoot you."

Christy Ring: "Ye might as well. Ye've tried everything else."

An irate County Board Official: "Where's your pass?"

Christy Ring (jumping over the stile instead of displaying his pass as he went into a match): "I don't have it."

"But Christy, you ought to have. You won no less than eight All-Ireland medals."

"And if I hadn't been carrying passengers like you, I'd have won at least eight more!"

"They haven't come to see you umpiring, they have come to see me hurl."

CHRISTY RING AFTER A CLASH WITH AN UMPIRE

"F-f-f-f**k you Lynch. Try that again an' there'll be a f-f-f-f**kin by-election."

TONY REDDIN HAD SOMETHING OF A SPEECH IMPEDIMENT AND DURING THE WHITE HEAT OF A CORK VERSUS TIPP CLASH JACK LYNCH CHARGED INTO REDDIN AND IN THE PROCESS BUNDLED BOTH OF THEM INTO THE NET

"If I had the ball they have today I'd drive it to fuc**n Doora."

FORMER CLARE GOALIE BEMOANING THE DEMISE OF THE OLD SLÍOTAR

"I think they can improve on their 100% record."

BRIAN WHELAHAN

"If Eoin's shot had gone in, it would have been a goal."
TONY BROWNE

"I am a firm believer that you have to score more than the other team if you want to win."
HENRY SHEFFLIN

"If a team scores early on: it often takes an early lead."
DJ CAREY

"You cannot possibly have counted the number of passes Kilkenny made; but there were eight."
TOMÁS MULCAHY

"Ah sure, Daly you can't score a point and what's worse you can't fuc**n even pull a pint!"
LIMERICK FAN AFTER PUBLICAN AND LEGENDARY CLARE PLAYER ANTHONY DALY MISSED A LONG-RANGE FREE

TEN

Amongst Women

It is a sign of the times that female icons are increasingly prevalent in the world of Gaelic games. Hence a fan's observation after the 2007 hurling quarter-final draw when the Déisse were paired with the Rebels yet again: "It's like an episode of *Buffy the Vampire Slayer* for Waterford. What will it take to kill off Cork?"

For generations though it seemed that the only role for women in the GAA was to make tea and sandwiches and wash dirty jerseys and togs. A quote from a male chauvinist pig encapsulates the problem: "Women playing hurling should treat it as a matter between playing consenting females in private."

Of course this marginalisation of women in sport was not unique to the GAA. Accordingly, before we consider ladies football it may be illuminating to establish the wider context by briefly considering the experience of women involved in sport as a whole. Unfortunately women often get a hard time from male sportswriters in all sports. Hence Brian Glanville's comment, "A woman playing football is like a dog walking on its hind legs. It is not done well but you are surprised to find it done at all."

It's Just Not Cricket

To outsiders cricket is simply a strange social ritual, with the most bizarre and incomprehensible rules, many lengthy tea-breaks and an obsessive desire to ruin countless pairs of white trousers. This may be why the Duke of Edinburgh, when asked if he had any complaints about modern cricket in 1987 said, "I only wish some of the players' trousers fitted better."

Cricket is often considered to be a bastion of male chauvinist pigs. Hence the notice on many cricket clubs, 'No Dogs or Women'. For over 200 years the MCC, Marylebone Cricket Club, adhered to a 'No Women' policy. This led to no women members, no women in the Pavilion on match days and no women guests allowed. In 1988 a poll was taken on the revolutionary suggestion to allow women into the pavilion as guests. Not surprisingly the motion was overwhelmingly defeated. Three years later another motion was put to members. This time the question was: "Should women be allowed to join the 20-year waiting list?" Again this innovative proposal was roundly rejected. Many people might have misgivings about these chauvinistic tendencies. The MCC, though, rejoice in it.

Golf too continues to have problems regarding giving women equal treatment including denying women access to golf clubs. Some women though have not taken this lying down. Mrs Elspeth Mustard, Secretary to the Secretary at Muirfield, Edinburgh, said to an American woman visitor, "I am sorry we don't allow ladies in the clubhouse."

The American woman replied, "Then, what are you?"

Gaffes

Sometimes women caused unexpected ripples in sport. During Harold Macmillan's time as Prime Minister of England he received a grave message about a diplomatic disaster during a Parliamentary recess. BBC radio reported the event as follows, "These dismal tidings were delivered to the PM on the golf course where he was playing a round with Lady Dorothy." The words read fine in print but when spoken the sentence took on a very different connotation!

Little Women

In Japan many of the caddies are women. Many are very attractive. It is not unusual for a pro to kiss his caddie. According to legend one guy started out playing alone with his caddie. By the 9th hole they were engaged and when they finished on the 18th they had a foursome.

When A Woman Loves A Fan

Women often suffer at the hands of sports-mad husbands. Elsie Revie, wife of the legendary Don, Manager of Leeds United, often told her two children, "See that man walking past the window. That man's your father."

In American football the quarter-back is the pivotal position and the glamour boy. As a result he is invariably the subject of a lot of female attention. Joe Namath, New York Jets quarterback, spilt the beans, "When we won the League Championship, all the married guys on the club had to thank their wives for putting up with the stress and strain all season. I had to thank all the single broads in New York."

Asked why he got married at 11 am, Paul Hornung of the Green Bay Packers said, "Because if it didn't work out, I didn't want to waste the whole day."

Henny Youngman famously said, "The first part of our marriage was very happy. The problem was the second part of the marriage. That began on the way home from the ceremony."

Dorothy Shula, wife of Miami Dolphins football coach, Don Shula said, "I'm fairly confident that if I died tomorrow, Don would find a way to preserve me until the season was over and he had time for a nice funeral."

Dedicated Followers Of Fashion

Fashion sense is a major item of concern in horse racing. In 1971 the authorities decreed that ladies in hot pants would only be allowed to enter the Royal Enclosure at Ascot if the 'general effect' was satisfactory.

The Trail Blazers

Historically, this marginalisation of women in sport is of course a reflection on the wider society and can even be traced back to Biblical times. Adam was out walking with his sons Cain and Abel one day. When they passed the Garden of Eden, which Adam and Eve had once called 'home', one of the boys asked, "What's that?"

"That's where your mother ate us out of house and home," Adam replied.

Thankfully in recent years women have finally made their mark in sport. One of boxing's most influential figures in the last generation has been Eva Shain. The Jewish grandmother who lives in New Jersey in the United States made history in 1977 when she became the only woman to judge a Muhammad Ali world title fight. Ali was defending against Earnie Shavers at Madison Square Garden. At the press conference after the fight, Ali was asked if he had been aware that one of the judges was a woman.

"No," he replied.

"What did you think of this lady judge?" a journalist asked.

"How did she score the fight?" Ali inquired.

"She scored it 9-6 in your favour."

"She's a mighty fine judge."

In 1985 Eva was inducted into New Jersey's Boxing Hall of Fame. Ali was the star guest at the function. Turning to the lady judge, he asked in confidential tones: "Doesn't all that blood bother you?"

"No," Eva replied.

"Why not?" Ali wondered.

"Because it's not mine."

Champion

One of the women who did most to ensure that women got equal treatment was nine time Wimbledon Champion Martina Navratilova. In 1978 she announced her arrival on to the centre stage by defeating 'Chrissie' (Chris Everet) to win her first Wimbledon. The fans responded with either coolness or outright hostility. To her critics she was not, to put it at its mildest, physically attractive, verbally rude, mentally aggressive and worst of all she was 'sexually deviant'. She had the honesty and courage to declare herself gay when from a purely commercial point of view, in terms of sponsorship deals, she would have been better served by denial. Hence the voices in the Wimbledon crowd shouting, "Come on Chrissie, I want a real woman to win." One commentator described her as "arrogance to panic with nothing in between". Another claimed that: "The real problem with Martina is that she never dated Burt Reynolds."

Martina took it in her stride and was even funny with it.

"Martina, are you still a lesbian?" inquired a male sportswriter.

"Are you still the alternative?" she replied.

Surprisingly the tennis sisters do not always show much sisterly love. Pam Shriver never really fulfilled the potential she showed when reaching the final of the U.S. Open at the age of 16 in 1978. The main successes of the woman from Baltimore, Maryland, were achieved as Martina Navratilova's doubles partner. She is, though, the queen of the after dinner speeches. During the latter stages of Chris Everet's difficult pregnancy Pam told her peers: "I've just spoken to Chris and she wants you to know that she will not be appearing nude á la Demi Moore on the cover of *Vanity Fair* magazine. But she said she would be would be willing to appear on the cover of *Inside Women's Tennis*, if it would improve circulation – the magazine's and hers." Her humour can also have an edge to it. In her book, *Passing Shots*, she remarked that all three Maleeva sisters reminded her of basset hounds because of their doleful expressions. Accordingly, she called them 'Boo', 'Hoo', and 'Boo-Hoo'.

Maybe it is for the cutting remarks like this that the queen of the grunters, Monica Seles was compelled to say: "I definitely have some friends who are not my friends."

Mighty Mayo

Ladies football reflects the more prominent role of women in sport. In fact ladies football is the fastest growing participation sport in Ireland. The most obvious symptom of the higher profile of ladies football is the players' involvement in prominent television advertising campaigns. This is reflected in a story of one Mayo ladies football player's search for a new job. At the end of a job interview, the Head of Human Resources asks her, "What starting salary are you looking for?"

Given the players high television profile, she decides to shoot for the moon, "I'm thinking of 125 grand a year or so, depending on the benefits package."

"Hmmmm. Well what do you say to six weeks paid vacation, 14 paid holidays, full medical and dental, and retirement funds that will match at 50%, and a company car leased every two years, say maybe a fine Porsche?" replies the interviewer.

The player gasps and says, "Wow, are you kidding?" "Yeah," agrees the interviewer, "but you started it."

The Bitter Word

Cora has made Mayo one of the most powerful forces in ladies football. The ease with which the Mayo ladies can win the All-Ireland is often contrasted with the problems the Mayo men have in emulating that achievement. Not surprisingly Pat Spillane has got in on the act. He famously said...

"The time has come for me to confound my critics and bravely admit that in the last five years Mayo have had one of the best teams I have ever seen – their ladies football team.

Last night I was struck by a very rare brainwave. I can now exclusively reveal that plans are well advanced for my new series about Mayo footballers. It is to be called 'Footballers' Husbands'."

Runaround Sue

Laois lady football superstar Sue Ramsbottom is perhaps the greatest ladies footballer of all time. Her bias was evident at an early age: "When most of my friends were besotted with Jason Donovan and Bros my two heroes were less likely pin-up material – Barney Rock and Colm O'Rourke!"

Given her role in the army Sue's freedom to publicly campaign on political issues is greatly curtailed. Down through the years many Irish people supported the Birmingham Six and the Guildford Four. Sue cast aside her inhibitions to publicly align herself with the, 'Free the Laois One' Campaign.

After they lost an All-Ireland the Laois side were really devastated. In the build-up to the game there was a lot of hype at home and they painted a Beetle in the Laois colours; blue and white, and they put all their names on it. They parked it as near as possible outside Croke Park the day of the match. The next morning they heard the car was missing. Then they discovered it had been impounded because the car was so old there was no point in paying tax on it for the day though it was insured. The Laois team were staying in a hotel in Lucan but they decided to go into town to try and get the car back. One of the biggest characters on the team, Lulu Carroll, made up a song which they all chanted:

> "Where's the Beetle gone,
> Far, far away
> The cops took it away."

It became a big media story and was discussed on Marian Finucane's show.

Sue's departure for army duty in the Lebanon in the 1990s coincided with a controversy in Roscommon over Malachy Byrne's opposition to a £900 grant from Roscommon VEC for the promotion of ladies football. The controversy was fuelled further as he sought to explain himself on Shannonside radio and he said: "I reckon that a lady or girl's body is too precious to be abused, bumped and humped playing football. Their bodies are not made for humps and bumps. They have their own natural humps and bumps."

All The Presidents Women

When Geraldine Giles was elected President of the Ladies Gaelic Football Association some of her friends joked about her new position, mindful of the fact that it is the fastest growing sport in the country. Accordingly, they circulated an account of an imaginary visit Geraldine made to Ireland's best known psychiatrist, Dr Anthony Clare. When she was settled comfortably on her couch, the psychiatrist began his therapy session.

"I'm not aware of your problem," Doctor Clare said. "So perhaps, you should start at the very beginning."

"Of course," replied Geraldine. "In the beginning, I created the Heavens and the Earth . . ."

Murphy's Law

Juliet Murphy captained Cork to their first ever Brendan Martin Cup in 2005 and went on to emulate the feat the following year. Before the All-Ireland Final her Armagh opponents floated a story about her. In this account Juliet was driving on the road to Cobh when a Garda car pulled alongside her. The Garda was astonished to see that she was knitting as she drove. Realising that she was oblivious to his flashing lights and siren, the cop rolled down his window and shouted, "Pullover."

Juliet rolled down her window and yelled back, "No, it's a scarf."

The Orchard Lady

After Ireland played Australia in the first test in the Ladies International Rules Series in 2006 the Irish team relaxed and soon a conversation developed about the merits of men. Armagh captain and centre half-back Bronagh O'Donnell said she wanted a man who would always be there for her, who she could shout at when she was angry and who would keep her company and entertain her when she was depressed. Bronagh works as an audiologist in Belfast and heard a woman a few tables away responding to her wish by saying: "She should just get a television."

ELEVEN

Chicks with Sticks

Camoige's most famous star is Kilkenny's Angela Downey. During an All-Ireland final Angela was goal bound when her opponent made a despairing lunge at her which caused Angela's skirt to end up on the ground. Undeterred Angela kept on running, smashed the ball into the net and then calmly returned to collect her skirt. Not surprisingly she has been immortalised in folklore.

I Gave My Wedding Dress Away

When Angela got married, she asked to wear her mother's wedding dress. The day she tried it on for the first time Mrs Downey was sitting in the living room as Angela descended the stairs. The gown was a perfect fit on her slim frame. Mrs Downey's eyes welled with tears. Angela put her arm around her. "You're not losing a daughter," Angela reminded her in time-honoured fashion, "You're gaining a son."

"Oh, forget about that!" she said with a sob. "I used to fit into that dress."

Make Haste

Shortly after she got married Angela and her husband went to the dentist. Angela said to him: "I want a tooth pulled, and I don't want an anaesthetic because I've got a big match in a few hours. Just extract the tooth as quickly as possible, and we'll be on our way."

The dentist was very impressed. "You're certainly a courageous woman," he said. "Which tooth is it?"

Angela turned to her husband and said, "Show him your tooth, dear."

Animal Farm

Angela has a passionate interest in animal welfare. At one stage she met a camoige player from, all of places, Cuba. She explained to Angela that camoige was a tiny, minority sport in Cuba but that the number one sport was bullfighting.

The horrified Angela said, "Isn't that revolting."

"No," the Cuban replied "revolting is our number two sport."

One day Angela took her dog to the vet. She said: "My dog's cross-eyed, is there anything you can do for him?"

"Well," said the vet, "let's have a look at him."

So he picked the dog up and examined his eyes, then checked his teeth. Finally he said, "I'm going to have to put him down."

"What? Because he's cross-eyed?"

"No, because he's bloody heavy."

One of Angela's favourite stories was about the dog who went into a hardware store and said: "I'd like a job please."

The hardware store owner said: "We don't hire dogs, why don't you go join the circus?"

The dog replied: "Well, what would the circus want with a plumber?"

Revealing Talent

A lot of strange things happen in club games. The strangest story must be about a camoige club match in Westmeath when Cullion had a man on their team about 25 years ago. What was stranger was that nobody noticed the difference until after the match. The headline in the local paper was: "WHEN IS A GIRL NOT A GIRL?"

This is not a unique situation. In 1936 in the run up to the Berlin Olympics the Germans were very confident that Daren Rachin was going to win the gold medal in the women's high jump. She finished fourth. In 1957 the reason for their confidence was finally revealed when it emerged that she was a he. In 1992 before the Olympic Games in Barcelona the 2,400 female athletes were tested. It was discovered that five of them were men. Four years later in Atlanta a similar number of athletes were tested. This time eight of them were found, on closer inspection, to be men.

What It Says In The Papers

The President of the Camoige Association is Liz Howard. In a previous life Liz became embroiled in a major controversy. Following Clare's victory in the epic Munster Final in 1997 Anthony Daly made a speech in which he articulated the feelings and motivations of all Clare players and supporters on that day. Daly had that uncanny knack of putting into words exactly what every Clare person was feeling and his comment: "We're no longer the whipping boys of Munster", captured perfectly the mood of the day. A massive cheer went up from the Clare supporters when he uttered these words.

To the utter consternation of everyone in Clare, Liz Howard, then the PRO of the Tipperary County Board, wrote in a newspaper article that the statement was 'conduct unbecoming'. Liz spent most of her youth living in Feakle, where her father was the local sergeant, so her comments hit a nerve, especially in her former home village. However, when she repeated this 'conduct unbecoming' theme two weeks later, the whole thing spiralled out of control. Other newspapers picked it up and it became the topic of conversation. Ger Loughnane wrote an open letter to Liz Howard and that's when the whole controversy really took off.

It finally spawned an amusing sequel when a man came to the door of Daly's shop in Ennis and said, "You shouldn't have said that."

Dalo replied, "What did I say?"

"Well, I don't know. But you shouldn't have said it."

Pin-Up Girls

A coach to a camoige club, that shall remain nameless, was bemused when all her players burst out laughing when she came into the dressing-room and announced, "All the girls playing in the Saturday friendly match will be pinned to the notice-board."

Motivational Ploy?

It's hard to know what exactly RTE commentator Jim Carney had in mind when he asked former ace Tipperary forward and later multi All-Ireland winning camoige coach, Michael Cleary: "Besides their performances on the pitch, what kind of qualities do these girls have that makes you want to spend so much of your time with them?" The mind boggles!

Tip Off

Kilkenny's terrifically talented two-some, Sinead and Tracey Millea, took a taxi with a few of the other players after an outing one evening back to the team hotel. The taxi-driver was a bit obese and was also 'hygienically-challenged'; with a less than enticing aroma emanating from his body. In addition he recounted a tale of woe about his lack of success with the opposite sex. After the camoige players paid their fare the taxi-driver asked, "How about a tip?"

Before anyone could even think of reaching to their pockets for a second time Tracey is said to have interjected, "Certainly. Start using a deodorant and you might have some chance with the women."

Choose Your Words Carefully

Joe Brolly's ability to tell it as it is doesn't always have the results he anticipated. He was in a hotel one evening when the venue was descended upon by a party of camoige players. Anxious to find out the nature of the occasion, he asked one if it was a hen party.

"No," she answered sarcastically, "it's a Weight Watchers' convention."

"Oh, not been going long?" he inquired casually. That was the moment she floored him with a cracking right hook.

Ah Ref

One Tipperary ace forward is wont to complain to referees. After a series of bad decisions from one ref, she approached him and said, "If I called you a stupid old goat who didn't know the first thing about camoige, what would you do?"

"I would report you and you would be in front of the authorities," said the ref.

"What if I didn't say it, and just thought it?"

"Well, nothing could be done about it."

"Okay," said the player, "then we'll just leave it at that, then."

Knock, Knocking On Heaven's Doors

Two former Cork stars, Sandy Fitzgibbon and Irene O'Keeffe, sitting at a bar counter, were reliving the latest game they had seen. After a brief lull in the conversation, Sandy said to Irene: "I wonder if there is camoige in Heaven?" Irene said that nobody knew for sure, but suggested that they should make a pact there and then that whichever of them died first would come back and tell the other. They both agreed and the pact was soon sealed with another round of drinks. Sandy died and the day after being buried she turned up at the foot of Irene's bed as arranged. Irene almost died herself with fright, but soon remembered the purpose of the visit. She sat up immediately, eager to hear the news. "Tell me quick," she said, "is there camoige in Heaven?" Sandy replied: "Well, I have good news and I have bad news. The good news is that, yes, there's camoige in heaven alright. But the bad news is that there's a game next Sunday and you're playing full-back."

R.I.P.

Two stalwarts of a camoige club in Kilkenny were distraught. One said, "Have you heard the bad news? Old Mary is dead. And to think she was going to play left-corner-forward for the Junior B team tomorrow."

"My God. That's awful."

"It's tragic! But wait a minute . . . Maybe we can get Peggy to fill in for her."

Surfing USA

On the All-Star trips romance often flourished as Irish camoige stars were eagerly pursued by misty-eyed Irish Americans hoping to marry a 'cailín' from the old sod. However, two of the less-worldly All-Stars on the quest for a holiday romance got one hell of a shock when they discovered that they had arranged a double date with two transvestites!

To compound their embarrassment the next night the two girls got very suggestive chat-up lines. The first got: "You know what; I'd look good on you." The second received: "Your eyes are like spanners. Every time you look at me, my nuts tighten." Doing the rounds of a nightclub one guy struck a blank with both of them using the line, "Tog out. You're selected."

Catty Women

As the daughter of the Tipperary great Len Gaynor it is not surprising that Ciara Gaynor became the greatest centre half-back camoige has ever seen. Given Tipperary's intense rivalry with Kilkenny the Cats have a story about Ciara which suggested that she could not match her great triumphs on the field, off it. On a team holiday to America they claim that Ciara met Stevie Wonder in a bar. Ciara told him about the wonders of camoige and in return Stevie filled her in on all the music greats like Michael Jackson. Stevie casually mentioned to Ciara that he played golf. When Ciara expressed surprise he told her that he had been playing for years. "But how can you play golf if you are blind?" Ciara asks.

"I get my caddie to stand in the middle of the fairway and call to me. I listen for the sound of his voice and play the ball towards him, then when I get to where the ball lands the caddie moves to the green or further down the fairway and again I play the ball toward his voice," explains Stevie.

"But how do you putt?" Ciara wondered.

"Well," says Stevie, "I get my caddie to lean down in front of the hole and call to me with his head on the ground and I just play the ball to the sound of his voice."

Ciara is incredulous and says to Stevie, "We must play a game sometime."

Wonder replies, "Well, people don't take me seriously, so I only play for money, and I never play for less than $1000 a hole."

Ciara thinks it over and says, "Okay, I'm up for that. When would you like to play?"

"I don't care – any night next week is okay with me."

The Write Stuff

Former Cork star Lynn Dunlea has become the best known pundit in camoige because of her work on *The Sunday Game*. It is said that in her youth she professed her desire to become a great writer. When she was asked to define 'great' she said, "I want to write stuff that the whole world will read, stuff that people will react to on a truly emotional level, stuff that will make them scream, cry, howl in pain and anger."

Subsequently she was offered a job working for Microsoft, writing error messages.

Check-List

When the Cork camoige team went on tour to America their midfield maestro Linda Mellerick was admiring the new Joyce Hall that had been built on a university campus.

"It's a real thrill to see that a great Irish writer like James Joyce is been honoured in this way." she said.

"Actually," said the guide, "It's named after Joshua Joyce. No relation."

The Cork camoige star was astonished. "Was Joshua Joyce a writer, also?"

"Yes, indeed," said her guide. "He wrote a cheque."

The Star Of The County Down

Mairín McAleenan made her senior debut for the Down camoige team in March 1986. She went on to win almost all of camoige's honours. She is a big admirer of Bernie Kelly, Liatroim Fontenoy's teammate who continued playing to a high level right through until well into her 40s. On the way to the Ulster Club Final in 1998, Mairín was reading a newspaper article on the match, and the journalist had put Bernie in the 'veteran' bracket and questioned the wisdom of playing her in midfield at such a high level of camoige. "Do you hear that, Bernie," she said to her, "they reckon here that you're past it."

Bernie's response was: "Huh. Past it. I'll be hurling for Liatroim when I'm fu*king ninety!"

Mairín's summation of another teammate Donna Greeran is also noteworthy: "Donna would rather be chased by a rotweiler than give away a score."

Start Spreading The News

Player welfare is a big concern for managers today. Cork manager Fiona O'Driscoll took the team for a holiday to New York. Because of a booking glitch they ended up staying in a place known for its high crime rate or in Cork parlance 'a very rough area'. Fiona was very worried about security. The first night she advised the players to place a chair against the door of their hotel rooms and stack their luggage against them. To complete the barricade, they put the trash can on top. If an intruder tried to break in, they would be sure to hear him. Around 2 a.m. there was a knock on Fiona's door. "Who is it?" she asked nervously.

"Honey," a woman on the other side yelled, "you left your key in the door."

TWELVE

Fans Forum

Of course the GAA has attracted its share of famous fans. Eamon deValera attended every All-Ireland final during his presidency – even though by the end of his reign he was almost totally blind. One of his latter day All-Irelands had a number of controversial refereeing decisions. The losing manager was asked for his thoughts afterwards. He observed: "Dev saw more of the game than the ref did."

The GAA's best known anorak is Bertie Ahern. As a Croke Park regular he is a keen champion of the sporting press. "I love reading the sports pages. At least you know what's in them is true, unlike the rest of the papers." Many of his utterances sound remarkably like a GAA manager: "If hindsight were foresight, there wouldn't be a problem." Some of his comments are as logical as a GAA pundit: "I would never condemn wrongdoing."

Old Rivals

One of the best source of comedy among GAA fans is the intensity of the feeling between rival fans. A case in point goes back to the 1980s and early 90s when Kilkenny's dominance ensured a bleak time for Wexford hurling. This was most obvious on the Wexford side of the New Ross Bridge, which separates counties Kilkenny and Wexford. It read, 'You are now entering a Nuclear Free Zone'. A Kilkenny fan added a message of his own, 'You've now entered a trophy free zone'.

In 1996 Liam Griffin led Wexford to the All-Ireland. Some Kilkenny fans couldn't handle the new hurling order. One story illustrates this. That Christmas a Kilkenny family went into Callan to do some Christmas shopping. In the sports shop the son picked up a Wexford hurling shirt and said to his twin sister, "I've decided to be a Wexford supporter and I would like this jersey for Christmas." His sister, outraged by the suggestion, slapped him on the face and said, "Go talk to your mother." The boy walked with the Wexford shirt in hand and found his mother, "Mummy dearest?"

"Yes pet?"

"I've decided I'm going to be a Wexford supporter and I'd like this shirt for Christmas."

The mother could barely speak with anger but eventually said, "Go talk to your father."

Off he went with shirt in hand and found his father, "Dad?"

"Yes son."

"I've decided to become a Wexford supporter and I would like this shirt for Christmas."

The father hit the son a thump on the head and said, "No son of mine will be seen in a yoke like that."

As they went home the father asked the son if he had learned any lesson that day. The son thought for a moment before replying, "Yes I have. I've only been a Wexford fan for over an hour and already I hate you Kilkenny f***ers!"

Them And Us

Not surprisingly the intensity of feeling between rival fans has spawned some memorable comments.

Among them are the following:

"Winning the All-Ireland without beating Cork or Kilkenny is an empty experience, but as empty experiences go it's one of the best."

TIPPERARY FAN IN 2001

"A Kildare supporters' help line has been opened. The number is 1800 1 nothing, 1 nothing, 1 nothing."

MEATH FAN AFTER BEATING KILDARE IN THE 2007 LEINSTER CHAMPIONSHIP

"Avoid excitement watch the Dubs."

LOUTH FAN

"The only suitable replacement for Tommy Lyons I can think that can live up to aspirations of Dublin fans is Merlin the Magician."

MEATH SUPPORTER

"The Down forward line couldn't strike a match."

Q. *"Why did Mick O'Dwyer climb the Eiffel Tower?"*
A. *"He was looking for forwards."*
Q: *"What do Meath footballers have in common with a
wonderbra?"*
A: *"Lots of support but no cup."*
Q: *"What do you say to a Laois man in Croke Park on
All-Ireland Final day?"*
A: *"Two packets of crisps please."*
Q: *"Who were the last two Westmeath men to play
midfield in the All-Ireland Final?"*
A: *"Foster and Allen."*
Q: *"How many intelligent Cork fans does it take to screw
a light bulb?"*
A: *"Both of them."*

*"To call Donegal lucky would be to call the Atlantic
Ocean wet."*

*"It's not a North-South thing, sure we're all the same –
it's six of one and 26 of the others."*

T YRONE COMIC KEVIN MCALEER BEFORE THE 2003 ALL-
IRELAND FINAL

Neighbours

The Longford-Westmeath rivalry is one of the most keenly contested in football as was apparent in the 2007 Leinster Championship. An old Longford fan was dying and when it was obvious that he had very little time left the local priest, a Westmeath man, was sent for. After the priest administered the last rites he asked the old man if he had any last wish. He was astounded when the man asked if he could join the Westmeath Supporters' Club. The priest though duly pulled out a membership card for the man and helped him to sign his name for the last time. When the priest left the man's seven stunned sons crowded around the bed and asked their father why he had made this extraordinary request. With practically his dying breath he said: "Isn't it better for one of them to die than one of our lads."

Westmeath fans get their retaliation in. Four surgeons are taking a coffee break. The first one says, "Accountants are the best to operate on because when you open them up everything inside them is numbered." The second surgeon says, "Librarians are the best: everything inside them is in alphabetical order." The third surgeon says, "Electricians. Everything inside them is colour-coded." The fourth one says, "I prefer Longford footballers. They're heartless, spineless, gutless and their heads and arses are interchangeable."

Everybody Needs Good Neighbours

Donegal and Monaghan 'enjoy' a great rivalry on the football field with Cavan and their fans are never slow to invoke the stereotypical image of Cavan people revealed in stories like the Cavan footballer who gave his wife lipstick for Christmas every year so that at least he could get half of it back.

One story they tell in this context is about the Pope. He had a very, very unusual blood type. The doctors could only find one person in the whole world who had the same blood type; Paddy O'Reilly the Cavan footballer. So Paddy donated a pint of blood and the Pope recovered. As a gesture of goodwill the Pope sent Paddy on €20,000. The Pope got ill four times in successive years after that and each time he got a pint of Paddy's blood and each time he sent Paddy €20,000. The sixth time he got Paddy's blood the Pope sent him only a holy medal. Paddy was devastated and rang the Vatican to ask why he got no money this time. The Pope's secretary took the call and answered, "Well Paddy you have to understand he has a lot of Cavan blood of him at this stage!"

That may be why Monaghan fans say that when the Cavan football team went on a short holiday the hotel they stayed at put their Gideon Bibles on chains.

The Winner Takes It All

For all their fanaticism, defeat and dejection is the inevitable diet of most GAA fans as the Championship unfolds each year. Some supporters, though, can still raise a smile on their darkest days when their wounds are still painfully raw:

"Kerry would have won if Meath hadn't turned up."

A KERRY FAN REFLECTS ON THE ALL-IRELAND SEMI-FINAL DEFEAT IN 2001

"Behind every Galway player there is another Galway player."

MEATH FAN AT THE 2001 ALL-IRELAND FINAL

"The Mayo forward line has ISDN. It still does nothing."

FRUSTRATED BALLINA MAN AFTER THE LOSS TO GALWAY IN 2007

"Poor Mayo, with no real method up front, resembled a fire engine hurrying to the wrong fire."

SPECTATOR AT THE INFAMOUS 1993 ALL-IRELAND SEMI-FINAL AGAINST CORK

"I think Mickey Whelan [Dublin Manager in 1996] believes tactics are a new kind of piles on your bum."

DISGRUNTLED DUBS FAN

"The natural state of Antrim football fan is bitter disappointment."

ANTRIM FAN

Mayo fan at 2006 All-Ireland: "If you take the defending out of the equation; we played okay."
Kerry fan: "If you take the assassination out of the equation; JFK and Jackie enjoyed that drive from Dallas to the airport."

"The Kilkenny players took their sleeping pills too late because they hadn't fully woke up until after the match!"

DEJECTED FAN IN 1966 AFTER RED HOT FAVOURITES KILKENNY SURPRISINGLY LOST THE ALL-IRELAND TO CORK

"Get away ya bleedin witchdoctor."

DUBLIN FAN TO HERBALIST SEAN BOYLAN AFTER THE 1991 SAGA

"Our defence was as effective as Joe Jacob's iodine tablets in a nuclear holocaust."

DUBLIN FAN AFTER CLARE'S DEMOLITION JOB IN 2002

"It was like thinking you have gone to bed with Liz Hurley only to wake up to the terrible realisation that you slept with Red Hurley."

LOUTH FAN REACTS TO CONCEDING A LATE EQUALIZER TO WICKLOW IN 2007

"What Billy Morgan needs most is a Bob the Builder set to help him rebuild his Cork team.

"A young boy's parents were getting divorced. The judge asked him: "Would you like to live with your father?"
"No he beats me."
"So you would like to live with your mother?"
"No she beats me."
"Well who would you like to live with?"
"The Kilkenny football team – they can beat nobody!"

Croke Park announcer: 'Fogra. Would patrons please note that for safety reasons, by order of the Gardaí, that drinks . . . are on the house?'
Fellow Tipp fans: Loud cheer.

TIPP FAN AFTER SHOCK 2007 ALL-IRELAND QUARTER-FINAL
DEFEAT TO WEXFORD

Last Will And Testament

A Clare farmer was making out his will the day after Clare lost to Waterford in the 2007 Championship. His solicitor was surprised at one of his clauses: "To Páidí O'Shea I leave my clown suit. He will need it if he continues to manage as he has in the past."

Another Clare fan joked after the match that Páidí was going to a fancy-dress party dressed as a pumpkin. He was hoping at midnight he would turn into a coach.

Full

On All-Ireland Hurling Final Sunday 2006, as Cork hurling fans braced themselves for what they hoped would be a three-in-a-row, two Leesiders were preparing to board the Luas in Ranelagh. As the Luas was already jammed to the roof; a Kilkenny fan shouted at them: "Hop on to the Calcutta express."

Security Conscious

Before Meath played Dublin in 2007 an anxious Meath fan boldly parked his car in Archbishop's House in Drumcondra. Just when he thought his troubles were over some of the Dublin fans started chanting at him: "We know where your car is parked do-dah. Do-dah."

The Wee County

This year a new rivalry emerged between Louth and Wicklow during the three games they played in the Leinster Championship. It would have meant so much to Wicklow football to have put one over on their more illustrious rivals. *Sky Sport* were asking people leaving the England match after their 1-1 draw to Brazil in Wembley if they were disappointed.

Fan: "Not at all, I'm Irish, I'm from Bray."

Reporter: "But would you not support England when Ireland are not playing?"

Fan: "No way."
Reporter: "Why not?"
Fan: "800 years of oppression."
Reporter: "Is there ever any time you would support England?"
Fan: "If they were playing Louth."

Blood Boilers

As countless phone-in shows have demonstrated few things excite the indignation of GAA fans more than referees. Every cloud has a silver lining because their naked animosity is occasionally channelled into moments of comedy:

Roscommon fan after the controversial 1980 All-Ireland final: "Hi ref, how's your dog?"
Ref: "What do you mean? I don't have a dog."
Fan: "That's strange. You're the first blind man I've ever met that doesn't have a guide dog!"

"He [the referee] wouldn't see a foul in henhouse."
Frustrated Sligo fan after the 2002 Connacht Final

"There are two things in Ireland that would drive you drink. GAA referees would drive you to drink and the price of drink would drive you to drink."

ANOTHER SLIGO FAN AT THE SAME MATCH

"The referee wet ape. He pulled out more cards than Steve McQueen did in the Cincinnati Kid."

DUBS FAN IN 1983 WHEN 12 MAN DUBLIN BEAT 14 MAN GALWAY IN THE ALL-IRELAND

Hard Men

Some GAA fans in the south are not very keen on the physicality they perceive in Ulster football. The great American sports writer, Red Smith said: "I went to a fight and an ice hockey match broke out." These fans claim that Ulster Championship matches remind them of Smith's line.

Accordingly, they tell a story told about the two grasshoppers who came onto the field before an Ulster final as the pulling and dragging started between the players on both teams. One said to the other, "We're going to be killed here today. Do you feel the tension?"

The other replied, "I do. Hop up here on the ball. It's the only place we'll be safe!"

Medical Miracle

Armagh fans were not happy with the way the Tyrone forwards, especially Brian Dooher would go to ground after any light physical contact and perish the thought might exaggerate the nature of his injuries. They started a rumour that after a particularly theatrical fall Dooher thought he was dead. When the Tyrone team doctor went on to the pitch he found it tough to convince Dooher he was still alive. Nothing seemed to work. Finally the doctor tried one last approach. He took out his medical books and proceeded to show the Tyrone captain that dead men don't bleed. After a long time Dooher seemed finally convinced that dead men don't bleed.

"Do you now agree that dead men don't bleed?" the doctor asked.

"Yes, I do," Dooher replied.

"Very well, then," the doctor said.

He took out a pin and pricked Dooher's finger. Out came a trickle of blood.

The doctor asked, "What does that tell you?"

"Oh my goodness!" Dooher exclaimed as he started incredulously at his finger. "Dead men do bleed."

Fandom

GAA fans are known for the sharpness of their tongue. The following selection provides the book of evidence:

"I was expecting a dictatorship of experts. Instead we have a dictatorship of idiots."

WATERFORD FOOTBALL FAN ON THE PUNDITS AFTER BEATING HOTLY FANCIED CLARE IN THE 2007 MUNSTER CHAMPIONSHIP

"John O'Mahony has given up football. He's just become Kildare Manager."

WASPISH GALWAY FAN

"The toughest match I ever heard off was the 1935 All-Ireland semi-final. After six minutes the ball ricocheted off the post and went into the stand. The pulling continued relentlessly and it was 22 minutes before any of the players noticed the ball was missing!"

MICHAEL SMITH

"There is nothing even vaguely intellectual about a Munster Hurling Final, yet a proper enjoyment of the game presupposes a sophisticated appreciation of the finer things."

DAVID HANLY

"If you put monkeys on to play they'd still pack Croke Park on All-Ireland Final day."

KILKENNY FAN

"Rugby is a sport for ruffians played by gentlemen, Gaelic football is a sport for gentlemen played by ruffians but hurling is a sport for gentlemen played by gentlemen."

ANON

"They wouldn't bate dust off a carpet."

KILKENNY FAN PREMATURELY DISMISSES GALWAY'S CHANCES BEFORE THE 2001 ALL-IRELAND SEMI-FINAL

"My definition of a foreigner is someone who doesn't understand hurling."

A UNIQUE CONTRIBUTION TO THE ASYLUM SEEKERS DISCUSSION

"Cork hurling games are like sex films they relieve frustration and tension."

JOE LYNCH

"Why are Limerick magic?"
"Because they can disappear for five minutes."

OFFALY HURLING FINAL AFTER THE DRAMATIC 1994 ALL-IRELAND FINAL

"A forward's usefulness to his side varies as to the square of his distance from the ball."

GALWAY FAN DURING THE 2001 ALL-IRELAND

THIRTEEN

Media Motormouths

Q: "How many GAA pundits does it take to change a light bulb?"
A: "None. They just sit there in the dark and complain."

GAA pundits are the people we love to hate – except on those rare occasions their prejudices resonate with ours. Yet they have become an integral part of the sporting landscape and folklore.

Bernard Flynn, Kevin McStay and Anthony Tohill are walking along when they come along a set of tracks. Flynn says, "Look at those bear tracks."

McStay says, "No they're squirrel tracks."

Tohill says, "No they're bird tracks."

They continued arguing until suddenly the train hit them.

Forgive Us Our Trespasses

Admhaím do Dhia uilechumhachtach
agus daoibshe, a bhráithre,
gur pheacaigh mé go trom.
A Thiarna, déan trócaire.

If you didn't understand those last four lines you have no chance of ever raising to even lowly office in the GAA. Those of you who did will recognise it as a prayer asking for forgiveness and mercy. Sadly given their propensity to put their feet in their mouths, this is the prayer GAA pundits have to say the most often!

Those Magnificent Men In Their Flying Machines

A man is flying in a hot air balloon and realizes he is lost. He reduces height and spots a man down below. He lowers the balloon further and shouts: "Excuse me, can you tell me where I am?"

Kevin McStay below says: "Yes, you're in a hot air balloon, hovering 30 feet above this field."

"You must be a GAA pundit," says the balloonist.

"I am," replies McStay. "How did you know?"

"Well," says the balloonist, "everything you have told me is technically correct, but it's no use to anyone."

McStay says, "You must be a GAA referee."

"I am," replies the balloonist, "But how did you know?"

"Well," says McStay, "you don't know where you are, or where you're going and you're in the same position you were before we met, but now it's my fault."

Anyone For Ices?

Tipperary football fans are not known for their affection for Kevin McStay given his comments about the role, or more precisely lack of role, for the so-called 'weaker counties' in the Championship. In retaliation they tell the story of the day Kevin approaches an ice-cream van in Roscommon and asks, "I'd like two scoops of chocolate ice-cream, please."

The girl behind the counter replies, "I'm very sorry, sir, but our delivery didn't come this morning. We're out of chocolate."

"In that case," McStay continues, "I'll have two scoops of chocolate ice-cream."

"You don't understand, sir," the girl says. "We have no chocolate."

"Then just give me some chocolate," McStay insists.

Getting angrier by the second, the girl asks, "Sir, will you spell 'van', as in 'vanilla'?"

McStay spells, "V-A-N."

"Now spell 'straw', as in 'strawberry'."

"Okay. S-T-R-A-W."

"Now," the girl asks, "spell 'stink', as in chocolate."

McStay hesitates, then confused, replies, "There's no stink in chocolate."

"That's what I've been trying to tell you," she screams.

After Galway emphatically beat Mayo in the 2007 Connacht Championship a Tipp fan sent in a text to *The Sunday Game* saying: "Now McStay you know what it is like to be from one of the weaker counties."

Navan Man

By profession Colm O'Rourke is a teacher in Saint Patrick's Navan but there is no question he is the most authoritative pundit on *The Sunday Game*. Although he is best known for his incisive analysis he has supplied many a good quote down the years.

My personal baker's dozen, in order of no importance of O'Rourkisms are:

Number 1

"Dublin were the nearly team in 2002 but as any farmer will tell you nearly never bulled a cow."

Number 2

"Joe Brolly always talked a great game. The problem was that he didn't always play a great one!"

O'ROURKE RESPONDS TO A JOE BROLLY AFTER DINNER SPEECH WHICH HAD A FEW DIGS AT THE MEATH TEAM O'ROURKE STARRED ON

Number 3

"If Adam was an Armagh footballer; Eve would have no chance. Instead of an apple, he would have looked for a banana, as this is on the diet sheet."

Number 4

"Benny Coulter has a left foot in the right place."

Number 5

"It's a play the man, forget about the ball type of game."

Number 6

"Who doses the bullocks in the country any more? The poor auld farmers. Every team needs a couple of farmers."

Number 7

"When your luck is out: your bullocks don't fatten."

Number 8

"If a fella was driving a load of straw through the Down defence, the Down backs still wouldn't be able to get their hands to it."

Number 9

"Down's plan last year was to kick the ball to Benny Coulter, and if that didn't work; to kick it even more to Benny Coulter."

Number 10

"Mothers kept a Mick Lyons photo on the mantelpiece to stop their children going too near the fire."

Number 11

"Ulster football is much more physical and that's before anyone breaks the rules."

Number 12

"The worst thing about the game was there wasn't even a chance of a row."

Number 13

"If you can't take a hard tackle: you should play table tennis."

O'ROURKE COUNTERS THE CHARGES THAT HIS MEATH TEAM WERE TOO PHYSICAL

Bernard's Choice

People think the live of a pundit in RTE is all about glamour. Not so. When you appear on a high profile programme on national television you are not near as pampered as people expect. On Bernard Flynn's first day in the job as a guest on *The Sunday Game* when meal time came he went to the RTE canteen for his evening meal. "What are my choices?" he asked. The man behind the counter replied, "Yes or no."

Observe The Sons Of Ulster

In recent years one of the most ongoing controversies about *The Sunday Game* pundits is the perception that the most high profile among their number have an anti-Ulster bias. One of their critics in this context is Ireland's finest sportswriter, the acclaimed documentary-maker; Peter Woods. The Monaghan native explains his passion for football in the following terms: "Why I love Gaelic football – all of life compressed into those 70 minutes . . . everything except death. Well almost everything because Ulster is different."

The main problem for the pundits is the way the top Ulster teams used the zone defence. Famously this was described as 'puke football'. After Tyrone triumphed over Kerry in the 2005 All-Ireland the pundits bemoaned the fact that Kerry were so badly served by the opposition they faced on the way to their final. Peter's solution to this problem was certainly original: "The logic of all this is overwhelming . . . for Kerry to compete against an Ulster team they must play in Ulster. Look on the upside – the Ulster Council's policy of appeasement of moving the Ulster Final to Dublin – has failed; we're still not liked down here. The Monaghan County Board want to redevelop Clones. With Kerry in Ulster there could be more games for the pundits to travel to North of Ardee, more rainy days in Clones, the chip wrappings fluttering about their ankles, traffic backed up on every road out of the town. Hell even AA Roadwatch would have to take notice. But the clincher is . . . just imagine what a boost Kerry would give to the Love Ulster Campaign."

His view of the pundits is also unique: "So perhaps I shouldn't be surprised when football pundits cast Joe Kernan and Micky Harte as twin Voldemorts, bent on raiding South and razing those citadels of fair-play and champagne football in Kerry and Dublin – their only real opposition those pundits, arraigned behind Pat Spillane, cast as 'Mad Eye' Moody and an uneasy Colm O'Rourke – given Meath's record – as 'Severus Snape', a foot in one camp and a toe in the genetic pool of the other. And there's Joe Brolly, one of our own, severely conflicted, glasses glinting like Harry Potter."

Earley To Rise

Former Roscommon star Paul Earley is a regular analyst on Setanta television. However, in a previous incarnation he was a regular presence on *The Sunday Game*. One of his best moments came after the 1988 All-Ireland semi-final when Mayo, managed by John O'Mahony, put up a credible showing before losing to mighty Meath. At the end Michael Lyster asked Earley: "Will Mayo be back?" Quick as a flash Paul replied: "I hope not!"

Prison Break

A journalist with *The Irish Times* was writing a feature about prison life in Mountjoy Prison and was interviewing one of the prisoners.

"Do you watch much television here?"

"Only the analysis on *The Sunday Game*," the inmate said.

"That's too bad." the reporter said, "But I do think it's nice the governor, John Lonergan, lets you watch that."

"What do you mean, nice?" the inmate said. "That's part of the punishment."

Dunne Deal

A great champion of hurling was the late Mick Dunne; father of newsreader Eileen. In 1949 Mick joined *The Irish Press* as junior librarian before quickly graduating to and becoming a Gaelic games correspondent and later Gaelic Games Editor of the Sports Department. He was well able to tell stories against himself about his time on the paper. He once sat in a hotel having his breakfast the morning after a Munster final and two tables away he could hear two men dissecting his report on the match. Their remarks weren't very complimentary. Later that morning he stopped for petrol at a small shop outside Thurles. As Tipperary had lost heavily the previous day the shopkeeper was still in foul humour. He asked Mick if he had been at the match. When Mick replied in the affirmative the shopkeeper went into a lengthy analysis of why Tipperary lost and then proceeded to ask Mick if he had seen, "what that f***ing bast**d Mick Dunne had written in *The Irish Press*." When Mick politely replied that he was aware of the contents of the article, the shopkeeper launched into a vicious tirade about Mick's knowledge of hurling and cast a number of doubts on his parentage in the process. Mick made no response until the very end when the shopkeeper said, "I bet that fella's getting a fortune for writing that rubbish. Tell you what, although I hate him; I wish I had his money."

Mick calmly paid him for the petrol and said, "Well you've just got £5 of it."

Radio Daze

Seán Óg O'Ceallacháin is a national treasure. In his office in RTE one day Seán took a call from a member of the public. The conversation unfolded as follows:

"Is this Seán Óg?"

"It is indeed."

"Seán Óg O'Ceallacháin?"

"The one and the same?"

"Off the radio?"

"That's me!"

"Sure what the fu*k would you know about soccer?"

Me And Jimmy Magee

In the pantheon of Irish sport special place is reserved for Jimmy Magee. No less a diplomat than a great broadcaster, he has a great flair for handling Dublin fans.

"Jimmy," an anxious Dublin fan desperately seeking assurance before the replay against Meath in 2007, "do you think we still have a great team?"

"Ah, my good man," Jimmy replied with the utmost sincerity, "'Great' is not the word to describe it!"

On The Air

RTE licence payers fork out significant sums each year to be entertained. RTE's Gaelic Games coverage takes this mandate seriously as the following compilation reveals:

"They've lost nothing today – except pride and, of course, the Connacht title."

MARTY MORRISSEY

"Meath are like Dracula. They're never dead til there's a stake through their heart."

MARTIN CARNEY

"There won't be a cow milked in Clare tonight."

MARTY MORRISSEY AFTER CLARE WON THE 1992 MUNSTER FINAL

"Lovely piece of whole-hearted fielding. Mick O'Connell stretched like Nureyev for a one-handed catch."

MICHEÁL O'HEHIR

"And here comes Nudie Hughes for Nudie reason."

MICHEÁL O'HEHIR

"Remember, postcards only, please. The winner will be the first one opened."

THE LATE LIAM CAMPBELL

"The Ulster Championship makes the Colosseum look like a bouncy castle at a kid's party."
TONY DAVIS

"If you didn't know him, you wouldn't know who he was."
CELEBRITY JIGS AND REELS STAR PAUL CURRAN

"An easy kick for Peter Canavan but, as everybody knows, no kicks are easy."
MARTIN CARNEY

"Identify the Derry captain. Anthony Hopkins, Anthony Clare or Anthony Tohill."
SUNDAY GAME COMPETITION

> *"It's time for Donegal to step up to the plate and come out of the closet."*

TONY DAVIS AS THE JOY OF A FIRST NATIONAL LEAGUE TITLE IN 2007 FAILS TO LEAD TO CHAMPIONSHIP GLORY

Trom Agus Eadrom

Roscommon fans will never forget the night before the All-Ireland Final in 1980. Kerry's Jimmy Deenihan was interviewed, by telephone, from the team hotel by Liam O'Murchú on RTE's special *Up For The Match* programme. Liam asked Jimmy: "An raibh tú ag feachaint ar an clár?"

He replied: "Ní raibh. Bhíomar ag feachaint ar *Match of the Day*."

Apparently the Roscommon players were watching in at the time and got a great laugh from Jimmy's answer. Mind you it was probably the only laugh they got that weekend!

The Bare-Faced Cheek

Given the penchant for nude pool among his Senior County players Tom Mullaney, Secretary of the Roscommon County Board, showed a flair for double entendre in his appraisal of the disciplinary measures, "As a group all players hang together or hang separately."

Writing in *The Irish Times* Keith Duggan's verdict on that Roscommon policy of 'total disclosure' when playing pool made for amusing reading, "Ah yes, the career of the Gaelic footballer can end in a flash. Just ask any of the

Roscommon Senior players. It will take many, many years before a Roscommon senior manager can stand before his team in the dressing-room and bellow the traditional GAA rallying cry, 'Show them yez have the balls for it lads'."

Float Like A Butterfly, Sting Like A Bee

Of course one of Ireland's biggest ever sporting occasions was held in GAA Headquarters. On July 19, 1972 it took Muhammad Ali eleven rounds to defeat an ex-convict from Detroit; Al 'Blue' Lewis, at Croke Park. The fight itself was unremarkable but it was a wonderful occasion, particularly after Ali announced that his maternal great-grandfather Abe Grady had emigrated from County Clare over a century before. As part of the build up to the fight Ali met the Taoiseach, Jack Lynch, who informed the pugilist that despite his busy schedule he hoped to make it to the fight the following Wednesday. Ali replied, "Since you're a busy man, I guess I'll get it over quickly."

"Ah sure, that would spoil it."

"Well in that case, I'll let Lewis stay in the ring for more than one round."

"I might get in there for a few rounds myself and keep things going," said Jack.

For Ali his Irish adventure was a bit of a culture shock. On his second day in the country he rang his publicist, Harold Conrad, "Hey, Hal?" said Ali, "Where are all the niggers in this country?"

"Ali," replied Conrad, "there aren't any."

Ali's press conferences before the fight were never less than memorable. At one point he caught the journalists on the hop when, out of the blue, he asked, "What were the last words the Lord uttered at the Last Supper?"

There was silence as the hacks present were not known

for their theological expertise. Ali answered his own question, "Let every man pick up his own cheque."

Although the fight itself did not live up to the frenzied anticipation it created, one journalist was heard to remark, "After this performance all we can do is rename the place Muhammad Alley."

Meejah Moments

Inevitably pundits and the Fourth Estate have their quota of quotable quotes:

"Gaelic football is like a love affair – if you don't take it seriously: it's no fun; if you do take it seriously: it breaks your heart."

PATRICK KAVANAGH

"Brian, in years to come GAA people will be sitting around their fires and they'll be talking about the great wing-backs of all time and you know something Brian, when they do: you won't even get a mention."

JIMMY MAGEE GIVING THE TEAM-TALK TO BOOST MORALE BEFORE A JIMMY MAGEE'S ALL-STARS TO HIS WING-BACK; FR BRIAN DARCY

"Is the ref going to blow his whistle? No, he's going to blow his nose."

COMMENTATOR ON KILKENNY FM

"Frank [The Cork County Secretary] Murphy: The comb-over who rules the world."

TOM HUMPHRIES

"Let's pick the team first and we'll sort out the terms of reference later!"

A JOURNALIST'S APPROACH TO THE SELECTION PROCESS FOR THE ALL-STARS TEAM

Garret Fitzgerald on the canvas trail in 1981 when he posed for a photo opportunity swinging a hurley: "I've always wanted to play hurling so I thought it would be a good thing to learn the rudiments of the game."
Interviewer: "So have you learned much?"
Garret (attributed): "Yes I have. How to swing a cue."

"The ruin has rained the game."
FORMER ARMAGH GREAT JIMMY SMYTH

"He was like a gun-fighter roaming the streets without his gun."
CON HOULIHAN

"There have been games this summer when if you wanted interesting viewing you would have been better off watching The Angelus."
CON HOULIHAN

"He was like a woman who smells a cake burning."

CON HOULIHAN ON PADDY CULLEN'S FRANTIC EFFORT TO KEEP
THE BALL OUT BEFORE MIKE SHEEHY'S FAMOUS GOAL IN THE
1978 ALL-IRELAND FINAL

"Mayo have more baggage than a hotel concierge."

DAMIAN LAWLOR

"He has the face of a man that is not always given to clean living."

JOE BROLLY, ABOUT CORK PLAYER NOEL O'LEARY

FOURTEEN

The Golden Voice

Micheál Ó'Muircheartaigh is one broadcaster who is universally loved. He is completely free from the pretension associated with many of his colleagues. Not for him was the nickname given to one of his peers – 'The ego has landed'.

Micheál has carved out a unique place in the affections of Irish sport lovers over the last 50 years. The most mundane of matches come alive in his commentary. Everything he says into his microphone is informed by a passion that is as basic to him as breathing. His commentaries are famous for the richness of their texture, abounding with references that delight and surprise like: "One from the hand: one from the land." (Micheál's verdict on Mark Vaughan's varied free-taking style in the 2007 Leinster Final).

The former Kerryman of the year was born in Dún Síon, near Dingle, in Kerry. He paints a picture of an idyllic childhood growing up on his parent's dairy farm. The fourth of eight children, the young Micheál loved riding the horse, bringing the milk to the creamery and being by the sea.

His style is unique. Hence Jack O'Shea's comment: "He [Micheál] can take the ball from one end of the field to the other with just the players' occupations."

The School Around The Corner

Before going full time into broadcasting, Micheál worked as a teacher. In an interesting insight into teacher education he was once told that in the 1950s there were just four lessons you needed to become a teacher in Ireland:

1. The history of Irish education was the hedge school.

2. Teaching Methods – always, always, always use a blackboard.

3. School Organisation – Never build a school beside an open sewer or dung hill.

4. Educational Psychology – Make sure to get the pupil outside the classroom before they wet the floor.

The Sport Of Kings

In his broadcasting career Micheál has found evidence that if horse-racing is the sport of kings; greyhound racing is the sport of princes. One of his coups was to become the first person to interview a British Royal, Prince Edward, on RTE Radio. As joint owner of Druid's Johnno; Prince Edward was celebrating his semi-final victory in the English Greyhound Derby at Wimbledon. Micheál stepped up and asked in his velvety soft tones, as only he can, "Now tell me, Prince."

Larger Than Life

Micheál loves the great personalities of Gaelic games. In conversation with this author he observed:

"Characters are good for sport. There were a lot of characters in the old days in Gaelic games when there were no managers and players were individuals. Nowadays with managers controlling players and not allowing them to talk to the media, characters are not as plentiful as they once were. If you think of the great Dublin team who arrived on the scene in 1974 you would have to say that they were a lot of characters on that team, none more so than Jimmy Keaveney and also people like Paddy Cullen and Tony Hanahoe. In the olden days there were great characters like the Gunner Brady of Cavan. I think even his name was one of the reasons that he had this aura that surrounded him and also from that side Bill Doonan was as interesting a character as I ever met. Another character was Paddy Prendergast from the great Mayo side of 1950 and 1951. Paddy Carney, also from that side, was a wonderful character. Sometimes he would even hold up the ball to show to the crowd and usually it went over the bar. He had a little bit of arrogance but he also had the skill to match.

When you think of the Kerry team they had great characters like Eoin Liston, Páidí O'Sé and Jack O'Shea. I remember the Munster Final of 1993 for a particular reason. Jack O'Shea was the captain and I was training Jacko and the Kerry lads in Dublin. Kerry had won the Munster Final from 1975 and in 1983 most people expected them to win again. I travelled to the match with Jacko and we had worked on his victory speech and we were very happy with it. The only problem was Kerry lost the match because of a late Tadhg Murphy goal. Jacko's great speech was never made!

But there was another twist to the story. Kerry forgot to bring to the Munster Cup with them and it was only quick thinking by Frank Murphy, the Cork Secretary that saved the day. He went into some press in the back and found some cup. I think it was the Cork Junior Championship trophy. That's the cup that was presented to the Cork

Captain, Christy Ryan, but I don't think anyone noticed!

In the modern game, Joe Brolly is a wonderful character. He's a person that never really surrendered to managers. Joe is himself. I often heard managers giving out about him. That didn't worry Joe. Football and hurling are all about entertainment and Joe is an entertainer."

Oops I Did It Again

In the 1980s, after a mild heart-attack, Micheál was recovering from surgery when a nurse asked him how he was feeling. "I'm okay but I didn't like the four-letter-word the doctor used in surgery," he answered.

"What did he say," asked the nurse.

"OOPS!"

The Accidental Diplomat

As an innocent thirteen-year-old Micheál found himself standing on the sideline at a junior club match in Kerry when a melee broke out that would leave the Semplegate Eight controversy from May look like a harmless tiff between two little girls in a playground. Think Mayo versus Meath in 1996 and multiply by four, with the spectators bunched so close together on the centre of the pitch that they could hear each other's inner thoughts. The referee was not having a good day and Micheál gently said: "The advantage law is the best because it lets you ignore all the others for the good of the game."

May I Have Your Attention Please

Not surprisingly Micheál's services are constantly in demand to act as MC in GAA functions. He never ceases to entertain. One of his many stories is about the three

Monaghan fans travelling by train to a match in Croke Park. At the station, the three Monaghan fans each buy a ticket and watch as the three Cavan fans only buy a single ticket between the three of them. "How are the three of you going to travel on the train?" asks one of the Monaghan fans.

"Watch and learn?" replies one of the Cavan fans.

They all board the train. The Monaghan fans take their seats but all three Cavan fans cram into a toilet and close the door behind them. Shortly after the train had departed, the conductor arrives to collect the tickets. He knocks on the toilet door and says: "Ticket please." The door opens just a crack and a single arm emerges with a ticket in hand. The conductor takes it and moves on. The Monaghan fans are very impressed, so after the match they decided to imitate their football rivals on the way home. When they get to the station they buy a single ticket for the journey. To their amazement, the Cavan fans buy not even a single ticket. "How are the three of you going to travel on the train?" asks one of the Monaghan fans.

"Watch and learn?" replies one of the Cavan fans.

Once they board the three Monaghan fans lock themselves in one toilet and the three Cavan fans lock themselves into another one nearby. The train departs. A short while afterwards, one of the Cavan fans leaves the toilet and knocks on the toilet door where the Monaghan fans are locked in and says, "Ticket please."

All's Not Fair In Love And War

Another of Micheál's anecdotes concerns the Tipperary hurler who dumped one of his first girlfriends after she gave him an ultimatum: shave your moustache or lose me. He thought it was unfair because she had a moustache of her own!

One Moment In Time

As a GAA widow Micheál's wife was having a go at her husband. "Your whole life is Gaelic games," she moaned. "You never take me out, you never buy me presents. You're either at a match or watching games on the TV. I bet you can't even remember when our Wedding Anniversary is."

"Yes, I can," replied her husband, "it's the same date that I was first in Croke Park."

"Every rose has its thorns. Being away from home every weekend is not conducive to domestic bliss. All marriages are happy. It's the living together afterwards that causes all the trouble."

Micheál's wife accused him of loving Gaelic games more than her. "Yeah, but I love you more than soccer or rugby," he replied.

Not For Better Or Worse

A young Kerry footballer was in love with two women and could not decide which of them to marry. Finally, he went to Micheál for advice. When asked to describe his two loves, he noted that one was a great poet and the other made delicious pancakes.

"Oh," said Micheál's, "I see what the problem is. You can't decide whether to marry for batter or verse."

Pay Attention Carefully

To GAA devotees Micheál's golden voice is their abiding passion. This was probably most graphically revealed in the course of the All-Ireland. A man and his wife were making love. Suddenly she noticed something sticking in his ear. Not surprisingly she enquired what it was. He replied, "Be quiet. I'm listening to the great man."

Few people have done more to promote the whirr of the flying slíotar and the thrilling sound of ash against ash than the voice from Dingle who makes GAA fans tingle, Micheál. To shamelessly steal from Patrick Kavanagh, "among his earthiest words the angels stray."

His hurling commentaries have been enlivened with quotes like:

"I see John O'Donnell dispensing water on the sideline. Tipperary, sponsored by a water company. Cork sponsored by a tae company. I wonder will they meet later for afternoon tae."

"Stephen Byrne with the puck out for Offaly . . . Stephen, one of 12 . . . all but one are here to-day. The one that's missing is Mary, she's at home minding the house . . . and the ball is dropping I lar na bpairce . . ."

*"He grabs the slíotar; he's on the 50 . . . . he's on the 40
. . . he's on the 30 . . . he's on the ground.
Pat Fox has it on his hurl and is motoring well now . . .
but here comes Joe Rabbitte hot on his tail . . . I've seen
it all now, a rabbit chasing a fox around Croke Park.
Pat Fox out to the forty and grabs the slíotar . . . I bought
a dog from his father last week, sprints for goal . . . the
dog ran a great race last Tuesday in Limerick . . . Fox to
the 21, fires a shot, goes wide and left . . . and the dog
lost as well."*

*"A mighty poc from the hurl of Seán Óg Ó'Halpín . . . his
father was from Fermanagh, his mother from Fiji, neither a
hurling stronghold."*

*"1-5 to 0-8, well from Lapland to the Antarctic, that's
level scores in any man's language."*

The Pub With No Cheer

Like all true GAA fans Micheál was deeply saddened
earlier this year by the death of Jimmy Murray. The glory
years of Roscommon football came in the 1940s. "If we
have the ball: they haven't it," was their motto at the

time. Jimmy Murray's pub-cum-grocery in Knockcroghery is arguably the spiritual home of Roscommon football with all its memorabilia from the county's only All-Ireland successes in 1943 and 1944; both under the captaincy of Jimmy, including the football from the 1944 Final. The football survived a close shave some years ago when Jimmy's premises were burned down – as he once recalled to Micheál with mixed feelings:

"The ball was hanging from the ceiling and of course the fire burned the strings and the ball fell down and rolled safely under the counter. The fire happened on a Saturday night and when the fire-brigade came one of the firemen jumped off and asked me, 'Is the ball safe?' As I was watching my business go up in smoke the ball wasn't my main priority! But the fireman came out later with the ball intact. The next day I got calls from all over the country asking if the ball was safe. I was bit annoyed at the time that all people seemed to be concerned with was the safety of the ball and nobody seem to be too bothered about what happened to the shop!"

Magic Moments

Brendan Behan claimed: "Critics are like eunuchs in a harem: they know how it's done. They've seen it done every day, but they're unable to do it themselves." That may be true in the theatre but not so in GAA commentary.

The definition that I feel best sums some GAA pundits is the late Peter Ustinov's: "A critic is someone who searches for ages for the wrong word which, to his eternal credit, he invariably finds." If there is a wrong word to be found you can bet your bottom dollar they will find it!

Micheál, though, always seems to hit the nail on the head. He has left an indelible mark on the GAA landscape with a series of classic comments about football. Here are just a few:

"Danny 'The Yank' Culloty. He came down from the mountains and hasn't he done well.

He kicks the ball lan san aer, could've been a goal, could've been a point . . . it went wide."

"Colin Corkery on the 45 lets go with the right boot. It's over the bar. This man shouldn't be playing football. He's made an almost Lazarus-like recovery. Lazarus was a great man but he couldn't kick points like Colin Corkery."

"Teddy looks at the ball: the ball looks at Teddy."

"In the first half they played with the wind. In the second half they played with the ball."

"David Beggy will be able to fly back to Scotland without an airplane he'll be so high after this."

AFTER MEATH WIN THE 1991 SAGA OVER DUBLIN

"I saw a few Sligo people at Mass in Gardiner Street this morning and the omens seem to be good for them; the priest was wearing the same colours as the Sligo jersey! 40 yards out on the Hogan Stand side of the field Ciaran Whelan goes on a rampage – it's a goal. So much for religion."

". . . and Brian Dooher is down injured. And while he is down I'll tell ye a little story. I was in Times' Square in New York last week, and I was missing the Championship back home and I said, "I suppose ye wouldn't have The Kerryman would ye?" To which, the Egyptian behind the counter turned to me he said, 'Do you want the North Kerry edition or the South Kerry edition?' . . . he had both . . . . so I bought both. Dooher is back on his feet."